CW00621930

FREELANCE PHOTOGRAPHY

John Morrison

DAVID & CHARLES
Newton Abbot   London   North Pomfret (Vt)

For Chas and Casey

Acknowledgements
Many thanks to Malc Birkitt, Colin Leftley, Barry Hunter, Mike Wilson, Martyn Barnwell, William Cheung, Stephen Hyde, Simon Archer, Derek Sayer, Mick Rouse, Russell Boyce, Will Curwen, John Russell, R. Alison and Simon Warner, for allowing their pictures to be used and for helping with the 'Insight' interviews. All uncredited photographs are by the author.

British Library Cataloguing in Publication Data

Morrison, John
  Freelance photography
  1. Photography
  I. Title
  770'.28   TR145

  ISBN 0-7153-9009-2

Printed in Great Britain
by Butler & Tanner Limited, Frome and London
for David & Charles Publishers plc
Brunel House Newton Abbot Devon

Contents

Introduction

Photography can be an expensive hobby, especially if you are
seduced by the advertisements to buy every whizz-bang piece of
technological gadgetry. This book will help you, first, to make your
hobby pay for itself—not an inconsiderable feat—and then to spin a
decent profit. The advice is directed at reasonably proficient
amateur photographers who want the satisfaction of seeing their
pictures published, and who want that satisfaction crowned with
worthwhile pay-cheques.

Professional photography can, if viewed from the outside, appear
a rather glamorous way to earn a living. This glamour is an illusion
for most photographers, however, who soon find that long hours
and big overheads play a greater role in their working lives than
champagne or exotic locations. And those photographers who do
have a genuinely glamorous lifestyle have earned their rewards
through many years of hard graft. Professional photography is, in
truth, a very overcrowded profession. Many are called to express
themselves in such an essentially visual way, but few are chosen.
For every photographer who hits the headlines and the gossip
columns there are a hundred hardy souls beavering away in
primitive studios and darkrooms, producing pack shots for mail-
order catalogues and the like . . .

I'm merely suggesting that the amateur photographer has few
grounds for envying his professional counterpart. The professional

Hobbyist photographers are free to shoot the subjects they want, *when* they
want. The basic aim of this book is to show ways in which photographers
can carry on enjoying themselves, while having the further pleasure of
getting their pictures published and banking worthwhile cheques.

may have few opportunities to take the pictures *he* wants to take; more likely he is merely one more cog in a vast industry dedicated to the propagation of dreams and images. He has to compete with a great number of other talented practitioners for assignments and commissions, knowing that the maxim 'you're only as good as your last job' might have been invented for photographers. No matter that work to date has been satisfactory: one major cock-up is all it takes to lose a valuable client. It's a stressful occupation for which only the most dedicated need apply.

Amateur photographers, on the other hand, have no such pressures, apart from the guilt that arises from buying more bits of matt-black hardware instead of shoes for the kids. They can shoot what they want, where they want, when they want — given the obvious limitations of time, imagination and ready cash. The world, as Arthur Daley would say, is their lobster . . .

Unbiased Opinions

The trouble is that the amateur photographer generally has amateur critics, whose criteria for success or failure may go no further than appreciating 'a good likeness'. Anyone who has the facility to take a reasonable snap will have a certain kudos among family and friends. But if this same amateur has any pretensions to selling his work then he will have to show his portfolio to an impartial audience — one which is less likely to shower praise than to point up obvious defects.

Friends may be uncritically impressed with his photography; that is, after all, what friends are for. They won't carp about poor composition, questionable focus or poor colour balance, but these are precisely the points that a buyer of photographs will stress. By the time you've finished this book you should have a better idea how to improve your photography and then to sell it profitably. As the first salvo in this campaign let's dispense with the term 'amateur' whenever possible. With its connotations of inexperience and ineptness it renders a disservice to those who shoot pictures for pleasure rather than profit. So from now on it's just 'photographers', in the sure knowledge that pleasure *and* profit need not be mutually exclusive aims.

If a photographer can produce salesworthy pictures then a good secondary income is in the offing. If that income grows sufficiently large, and commissions prove plentiful, then he may consider taking up photography full-time. But that is not a step to be taken lightly: the bankruptcy courts are full of photographers who could not recognise their own limitations. The decision to change professions requires a great deal of thought. If there is the slightest doubt about your expertise as entrepreneur, marketing specialist, photographic technician, man-manager, picture editor, accountant and diplomat, then stick to your present profession and regard your photography as a rewarding and remunerative hobby.

Chapter by chapter you'll learn how to hone your photographic skills, edit your work ruthlessly and present it in a professional manner. You will be introduced to the people whose job it is to buy and commission photography. The potential markets for your work are fully detailed, with advice on how to tailor your work to their specific requirements. There is information — and probably reassurance — about the best 'tools of the trade'. You will, in short, be encouraged to shoot and market your pictures in a thoroughly professional manner, so that cheques soon begin to outnumber rejection slips.

THE MARKET-PLACE

The Freelance Approach

In photography you already have a satisfying hobby. Why risk disappointment and failure by trying to make a profit too?

Perhaps it presents a new challenge. If you have already become reasonably proficient in the art, craft and science of photography then you will have 'outgrown' the family album. You'll want to do more with your talents than knock up a few prints for family and friends. You may think that an exhibition — or a portfolio in a photographic magazine — will provide you with a larger audience. Neither of these ambitions will make you rich or famous, though both can be stepping-stones to more lucrative work.

It's always difficult to start from scratch, and a few tear-sheets from publications will help convince potential clients to take you seriously. Every time your work is reproduced, further commissions become more likely.

A part-time freelance photographer has to combine ambition with practicality, in the knowledge that many aspects of professional photography will be closed to him. Much can be achieved by working during evenings and weekends, but many clients require full-time photographers. That's why this book deals only with work that part-timers can realistically tackle.

The professional photographic magazines often print letters from disgruntled high-street photographers, complaining that 'cowboys' are depriving them of work. And it's true that inexperienced photographers can cause a great deal of heartache if they are hired to cover unrepeatable events such as weddings. But full-time professional photographers have no divine right to make a living; it's up to them to prove to their clients that the quality of their work will justify their fees.

They complain, too, that the same 'cowboys' operate by under-cutting the prices charged by the pros. There is some justification in this, since a pro may have a studio to keep up and many other expenses that the part-timer doesn't. But photography is both a profession and a hobby, and any pro worth his salt is able to convince clients that a truly professional service deserves a truly professional fee. Nevertheless, those same high-street photographers are only too happy to recruit amateurs when there are too many Saturday weddings to cover . . .

So, on the whole, proficient hobbyist photographers have no need to feel any guilt about taking on assignments or getting their pictures published, provided they charge something approaching the going rate for the job. Taking on work for chicken-feed does nothing for the photographer's own bank balance, or the profession of photography in general.

If, for example, you are offered a derisory fee for reproducing one of your pictures, it's your responsibility to negotiate a more realistic sum. If the client won't budge . . . don't deal with him. Too many part-time photographers sell their work too cheaply, perhaps on the basis that half a loaf is better than none. But it's a short-sighted approach to a long-term problem.

Marketing Skills

It's easy for an aspiring freelance photographer to believe that there is a 'mafia' of photographers who, between them, have the business sewn up. He may feel he is on the outside looking in, and cannot see a way to get his pictures published. In reality, however, there is no 'inside' and no 'outside' — only a vast number of different groups and individuals marketing their own skills. There is no secret password needed to get your work accepted, but talent is necessary, and perseverence, and a willingness to go about the task in a logical way. Most important of all, the people whose job it is to buy and commission photography have to be made aware that you exist.

No photographer can survive for long by waiting for the phone to ring. Work has to be chased, and a good deal of a freelancer's time should be spent in forward planning. Taking a good snap is merely one part of the business.

A commercial outlook can give a sense of purpose to a photographer. It's sad that so many hobbyists have more equipment than ideas, meaning that they take beautifully exposed pictures of uninteresting subjects. Once you take your camera outside the family circle, you need a better reason to carry on shooting pictures than merely to amass a few thousand more colour enprints. Selling pictures provides a rationale for spending money on film and

processing, since no one can hope to develop a good photographic eye if they only shoot a handful of films each year.

Shooting pictures with a particular market in mind has many benefits: you will be actively looking for photogenic subjects instead of just waiting for pictures to appear by magic — they seldom do. You will be planning ahead, thinking up projects, making useful contacts in the publishing business and generally using your skills with a camera in a satisfying way.

Whatever kind of photography attracts you, you will need enough self-confidence to ride the inevitable disappointments and learn from the equally inevitable mistakes. Freelance photography suits people who can motivate themselves, approach new markets and — to some extent — create their own work by coming up with a regular supply of picture ideas. You need to set yourself realistic and attainable goals.

Don't expect miracles; your early efforts are unlikely to bring you very much in the way of prestige or riches. On the other hand, don't set your sights so low that you find yourself working for peanuts. There are a number of publishing outlets that survive only by paying contributors fees so low that they barely cover the cost of film and processing. There are plenty of people whose desire to see their pictures in print outweighs their better judgement about pricing their work. If your photographs are worth publishing, then you deserve the appropriate remuneration.

Your local plumber won't come to sort out your burst pipes on the vague promise that you might reimburse him for the materials he uses. So there's no reason why even the most inexperienced of freelance photographers should help to bolster someone else's income for no more tangible reward than a picture byline.

For some reason that defies logical analysis, some people are just plain photogenic: they 'take a good photo'. Some folk look terrific in the flesh, but don't transfer well to film; others are unprepossessing to the eye but seem to come to life when photographed. This little girl belongs to neither category. She was unselfconsciously co-operative while being photographed *and* equally charming in the resulting prints. It's up to the photographer to get the best out of his subjects, but it does seem that certain photogenic people make this process ludicrously simple.

Picking the Right Market

The communications industry is vast — and getting bigger by the day. This is truly the information age, when images, words and statistics fly around the shrinking globe with dizzying speed. When an aircraft is hijacked in the Middle East, or election results are announced in some emergent African nation, the television news broadcasts bring us the stories and pictures 'as they happen', with the national press and magazines following close behind with more in-depth analysis and opinion.

It's a debatable point whether we are enlightened or merely confused by the plethora of information and imagery with which we are confronted. It's certain, however, that visual imagery is increasingly important in our lives: photographs can provide us with an immediacy of experience that words alone seldom can. New imaging systems can transmit pictures electronically, and the next decade will surely see these systems being dramatically refined and extended.

So is the end of 'conventional', film-based photography in sight? Will still video images make even our state-of-the-art cameras as obsolete as the blacksmith's forge? Probably not; you don't need to be a Luddite to see that there is yet a healthy future for film-based photography. In terms of image quality it is light-years ahead of electronically derived pictures, and is likely to have the edge for the foreseeable future. The two media will most likely work in tandem, as people come to realise their respective advantages and short-comings, in the same way that television and newspapers combine to give us a full picture of current events. After all, the painter Delacroix once exclaimed 'From now on painting is dead', on seeing a daguerreotype photograph for the first time: a statement which ranks alongside 'Man will never fly' in its misreading of the situation . . .

The sleepy little Northamptonshire village of Ashton comes alive every October, when the World Conker Championships are held on the village green. Many similar events help to raise money for charity and make a good day out — for spectators, participants . . . and photographers. Freelancers may find that local papers or magazines are interested in a package of pictures and words, even if the words are nothing more than extended picture captions. A little gentle humour is in order.

Crowds can make it difficult to get uncluttered photographs, though many events' organisers are more than happy to let photographers through crowd barriers and 'behind the scenes'. The use of a telephoto lens and shallow depth of field, as here, can isolate a single figure from a busy scene.

Painting and photography *have* had a rather stormy relationship over the past 150 years, but now there seems to be a truce. With their own individual strengths and weaknesses there is room for both. In the same way there will be complementary uses for new and old imaging technologies. Still video pictures will be wired around the world, bringing us the news, while film-based photography will continue to be used when the extra quality is needed and deadlines are not so pressing.

Freelance photographers should be aware of new developments in films, cameras, lenses, video, etc, while not being distracted from their primary goal of shooting and selling pictures.

Realistic Ambitions

There are a great many markets which the part-time freelance can reasonably aim to supply, and these are covered in the following pages. It is important both to have personal ambitions and to ensure that these ambitions are realistic. No part-time photographer, however gifted, is likely to be phoned up by an advertising agency and asked to shoot the pictures for a campaign to launch a major new product. When photography is combined with a nine to five job it is equally unlikely that the photographer will be able to respond to the everyday needs of national newspapers, whose deadlines are unrelentingly tight.

Magazines with a reputation for first-class photography cannot risk giving commissions to untried and untested photographers — it's just too risky a proposition. They will want to see photographers who already have a successful track record in editorial photography. It's an attitude of mind which offers little

Famous faces are always in demand, whether the shots are candids or taken — as here — with the subject's full co-operation. Of course co-operation in such situations may amount to nothing more than allowing the photographer a few minutes to get his shots. It is always a good idea to go in with one or two pre-planned picture ideas to fall back on, while looking out for locations and props that may already be available 'on site'. People who are often photographed may well be less than enthralled by yet another photo-session; their boredom threshold will soon be breached if the photographer takes too long to get his act together.

Here, ex-world champion Barry Sheene was happy to pose on a two-wheeler, travelling at a rather more sedate speed than the machines he was more accustomed to riding. (Photograph: Martyn Barnwell)

comfort to the photographer who is just starting out, though it becomes more understandable if you look through the eyes of an editor. After all, a botched job by an inexperienced photographer could play havoc with a magazine's schedule.

No jobs without experience, no experience without getting jobs — it's a frustrating Catch-22 situation, and one which can bring disillusionment to the most optimistic photographer. Yet it's a situation which most established photographers have had to face at one time or another. They have overcome the difficulties; so can you.

The first steps in selling pictures may be nothing more exotic than photographing the neighbour's children and selling them the prints. The local cricket team could be approached: a single team photograph is likely to have at least eleven prospective buyers. The next step could be the setting up of a simple home studio, allowing formal portraits to be shot with the minimum of fuss.

The best pictures from these early efforts should find their way into a portfolio, which is the photographer's shop window in the matter of finding work. The company he works for might want photographs for a brochure, or pictures of employees at work and play to enliven the in-house journal. As confidence increases and skills develop, the photographer can begin to look at more commercial outlets for his work.

He may approach magazines and trade journals with appropriate photographs he's already taken, try to get commissions or suggest his own picture and story ideas. Instead of commissions, his interests may lead him to shooting stock photography — marketing them himself or developing a business relationship with a picture library. Stock pictures have uses that range from advertising and promotion to books and magazines. Since stock pictures aren't actually commissioned, this may seem a rather risky branch of the photographic business. However, those photographers who develop a good understanding of the market will find that stock photography can be very rewarding.

Photo-Decor

There is a small, though growing, market for photographs as decor. At the top end of this market a small number of photographers can make a tidy income from selling original photographic prints, usually in limited editions. But the collectors' market for original prints is very small, at least in this country, and only a few photographers make realistic sales.

Posters are a different matter, since they can be bought in the high street for a few pounds. All kinds of photographs sell as posters — from the inspirational types of landscapes that come complete with a few effete lines of verse, to the ubiquitous shot of the tennis girl scratching her bum. This shot is apparently — and unaccountably — the best-selling poster of all time.

It can be satisfying to find that your pictures are being bought on pictorial merit alone. The same is true of postcards; they too can provide an outlet for particular kinds of photography. 'Art' postcards won't make very much money, but your name will at least be on the back of each one. And what better to use for your own personal correspondence than a card with one of your photographs on it. The poster and postcard market is very changeable; styles which are in vogue one year will look very passé in twelve months' time.

The public are obviously more willing to buy images to decorate their homes that are a little more sophisticated than a pair of winsome kittens peering out of a wickerwork basket. Not that these don't sell too; those photographers who can stomach such glutinous subject matter can make a good living supplying scenics and animal pictures for calendars and greeting cards. A list of these publishing markets appears in the *Writers' and Artists' Yearbook*.

There is liable to be quite a difference between the pictures a photographer *wants* to take and the pictures that will be most *profitable*. The photographer who shoots only for himself, taking little notice of market requirements, will find it hard to make picture sales. If, on the other hand, he ignores his own interests and preoccupations in search of saleable pictures then he is in danger of becoming just a hack photographer. His pictures won't have the 'sparkle' that attracts a picture buyer.

Magazines

The next time you wander into your local newsagent, make a rough tally of the number of magazines and periodicals on display. Even the smallest of outlets will have dozens of titles, while the major city-centre shops will stock hundreds. And all human life is there— magazines that cater for every taste, from antiques to zoology.

There are general interest titles; magazines that cater for individual hobbies, professions and interests; reading matter aimed at men, women, children and minority groups; periodicals that cater for those who follow or participate in all manner of sports. There are magazines with a long and distinguished history, and others which appear suddenly on the bookstands and, not long after, vanish equally suddenly without trace. Some have huge circulations and an assured future; some are virtually one-man operations published on a wing and a prayer. Despite the lure of television, video, teletext and other high-tech information media, the magazine format goes from strength to strength.

Take down a magazine or two at random and count the number of photographs used. You don't need a great head for figures to calculate that the demand for photography is enormous—a demand that is constantly renewed week by week, month by month. The magazine market is insatiable and freelance opportunities are many; the secret is to differentiate between those magazines which use their own staff photographers and those which — to a greater or lesser extent — use outside contributions from freelance photographers.

No magazine can survive on purely speculative contributions, whether from writers or photographers. Many editorial teams are self-sufficient, with writers, photographers, picture editors, proofreaders and other specialists producing their issues 'in-house', leaving the freelancer out in the cold. Other publications have but a skeleton staff and rely greatly on outside freelance sources for their material; if you can work with such magazines then a profitable relationship may develop.

A second glance at the magazines on display will further narrow down the options, since specialist knowledge will often be required of contributors. Food photography, for example, is a discipline that presupposes an immaculate photographic technique allied to the arcane skills of a food stylist. Perfection is the name of the game: every curl of butter, every scoop of ice-cream, every bubble in a glass of tonic . . . everything must present an idealised culinary dream. It's a branch of photography that requires a level of studio skills that are beyond the general photographer.

This is not to say that freelancers are excluded from such specialised work — merely that magazines tend to hire photographers who already have a good track record in their chosen speciality. Ambition is no fault, though the aspiring freelance will often find success more easily by lowering his sights slightly and aiming at a more realistic market for his photographs.

Leisure Titles

The likeliest chances of acceptance come from magazines devoted to hobbies and leisure activities. This is, so we are told, the age of leisure, and we are voracious readers of magazines about our own particular interests. Collecting, gardening, climbing, crafts and model-making are just a selection of interests served by excellent magazines. More ephemeral pursuits such as skateboarding and CB radio are covered by equally ephemeral publications, which exploit their subjects while the going's good and then vanish from the bookstands as soon as public interest wanes.

The freelance photographer has basically two ways of seeing his work in print: by submitting what he considers to be suitable photographs on a speculative basis, or by being commissioned by an editor to shoot new pictures. Speculative submissions, by their very nature, offer no guarantees to the photographer of either publication or payment. An editor may find them suitable for immediate publication, he may reject them outright or — perhaps the most frustrating option—he may offer merely to hold photographs on file 'for possible publication'.

Magazines find it very useful to maintain a file of pictures. It's a cheap and convenient insurance policy for those occasions when deadlines are pressing and 'filler' pictures are required to fill editorial gaps, or break up overly wordy articles. For the photo-

grapher, however, it can be disappointing to get what at first sight seems to be a favourable response, only to find that his pictures are languishing unpublished in a magazine's filing cabinet. While many photographers may be happy to leave black and white prints with a magazine, they should think twice before doing the same with colour transparencies. Leaving colour slides in somebody's file is a bit like keeping money under the mattress: there are always other options which will provide a better financial return.

Submitting filler pictures is a traditional way for hobbyist photographers to try and get their work in print. However, their pictures could lie unnoticed till doomsday without necessarily being used. Keeping photographers' pictures on file is convenient only for the magazine concerned; the photographers are effectively providing a cheap picture library, since payment is only forthcoming after publication. Even then, contributors' cheques are likely to be depressingly low.

On Assignment

Commissions are better, in which a contract is made between an editor and a freelance photographer for the latter to shoot a picture, or set of pictures, specifically for the magazine. Publication in these circumstances *is* guaranteed, as long as the pictures prove to be adequate. Never mind that the contract is only verbal — there just aren't enough hours in the day to be signing papers in triplicate. If you get the nod then you've got the job, your pictures will be published and you'll be paid a fee. And the time to negotiate that fee

Some freelance photographers worry about getting access to theatres, shows and concerts, and one or two advertisers in the amateur photographic press fuel these fears by offering spurious 'Press Cards' — for a fee. These cards aren't worth the paper they are printed on; better to seek permission from whoever is in charge, or bluff your way in.

For many stage events, photographers — accredited or otherwise — will face a ban on flashguns. Even if flashguns *are* allowed, suitable vantage points may simply be too distant for flashguns to be effective. The flashguns endlessly popping at major rock concerts demonstrate merely the victory of hope over experience! Theatrical photography pushes skills to the limit, with exposure problems, low light levels and shallow depth of field to contend with. Pushing film (ie underexposing and then overdeveloping) is one option, though this procedure will increase contrast and grain. Here, the photographer has overcome these problems in a characterful shot of comedian Alexei Sayle. (Photograph: Simon Archer)

— and allowable expenses — is long before you pick up a camera. Getting commissioned is an efficient way of working, since you know that your labours will be rewarded. Speculative submissions to magazines can take just as much time, energy and expertise as a commission, but may be simply and unsentimentally rejected. Receiving a few rejection slips may help to harden the resolve, though getting too many will prove ultimately disheartening and no great help to the bank balance. Working 'on spec' may be necessary for those with little or no track record in magazine work to back up their ideas, but it offers no long-term solutions.

Most magazine editors are more than happy to listen to constructive ideas from both writers and photographers. Proposals should be as detailed as possible, and accompanied by examples of your work, whether original photographs or tear-sheets of previously published material. Send your proposal by post, give the editor a chance to assess its merits, then phone him up. If you wait for the editor to respond by letter, then you might be waiting for ever. Better yet, discuss the idea face to face.

Coming up with your own picture ideas is more constructive than asking vaguely for work to be put your way. There are plenty of good photographers around who can respond to an editor's prompting; more welcome are good photographers who can generate ideas and carry them through on time.

Sticking to what you know

Few people can class themselves as genuine experts on a particular subject, but we all have interests and hobbies. A skill that may be second nature to you — car maintenance, perhaps, or prowess at do-it-yourself jobs — may be a source of admiration to another person. It seems to be a common failing to underestimate our own abilities. These abilities, however commonplace, can help greatly when first attempts are being made to get pictures published in magazines. Such is the proliferation of titles that your own interests will be catered for by at least one publication. Take these magazines as your starting points; your own knowledge of their subjects can be combined with a thorough investigation of their requirements.

Editors will obviously be able to brief photographers about their picture requirements, though most relevant information can be obtained by scouring a few recent issues. Magazines, like film stars, are continually undergoing face-lifts; cosmetic changes that are hoped will attract more readers and advertisers. It's important, therefore, that copies of the magazines you refer to are recent ones.

You can look at how many pictures are used in each issue, and what ratio there is between colour and black and white. There are still a number of magazines that use no colour at all, apart from on the cover. Many others have only a small allocation of pages on which colour can be used. Only the more upmarket magazines — and the Sunday newspaper supplements — can run colour on every page.

Check how pictures are used. Do they tend to illustrate features, or are they given prominence in their own right? How are they cropped? Are most in landscape or portrait format? Are they traditional and conventional in style, or reflecting more contemporary photographic trends? Are single images in evidence, or does the magazine prefer longer picture stories?

Where is the magazine pitched in the market? Does it have a 'popular' approach, or is it more highbrow? Is there a place for humorous and filler pictures? What kind of paper is it printed on? It's natural that magazines which treat photography seriously will use a higher quality paper, in which case they will demand a better standard of pictures — probably on medium-format film or larger.

Magazines both lead public taste and are influenced by it. It's one of the editor's jobs to make sure that a particular readership is identified for his publication, so that succeeding issues reinforce the title's position in the market. Photographers and writers have their own parts to play, but they must be aware of the editor's intentions. Otherwise they will submit inappropriate pictures, suggest unworkable ideas, and make a hash of commissions.

Commissions take many forms. An editor might ask the photographer to shoot a portrait to head an interview or personality feature. He may need a selection of landscapes aimed at accompanying a feature on the countryside. Another typical brief might be to shoot a series of pictures that give (as words alone never could) a step-by-step guide to some activity, whether it be potting plants, erecting a garden shed or perfecting a golf swing.

The jobs are as varied as the magazines themselves. Some require the photographer to link up with a writer; others might assume that the photographer himself is capable of stringing words together for text or captions. Alternatively, a writer can often be persuaded to shoot the pictures to illustrate his own article. A lot depends on the size of a magazine's budget. Some low-budget productions require freelancers to do virtually everything except sell copies on the street corner! Magazines with a reputation for fine photography to maintain will prefer to run to the extra expense of hiring both photographers and writers.

The good news about the majority of hobby and leisure magazines is that they are voracious users of both black and white and colour photography; the bad news is that their rates of pay vary from the adequate to the downright laughable. But what the freelance may lose in one-off fees he may gain in repeated sales of pictures which suit the magazine format. If the hobby is one with which you are familiar, then you will be more likely to produce saleable pictures.

Magazines devoted to leisure-time activities are all about people, so the most appropriate pictures show people engrossed in their particular hobbies. In this shot the photographer manoeuvred himself so that the diagonal lines of the pier supports echoed the stance of a lad using his metal-detector in search for old coins, jewellery and other relics.

Picture buyers in the editorial market have to be impressed by your talents, and a portfolio — preferably changed for each editor you see — is a prerequisite. Just as important, however, is your ability to produce adequate pictures in what may be difficult circumstances and deliver the goods on or before an agreed date. It's a time-consuming business to chase up irresponsible photographers when deadlines are pressing. You've got to convince an editor that you're up to the task; if *you* don't think you are capable of producing what the editor wants then you shouldn't accept an assignment.

Payments

The rates of pay offered by magazines vary enormously, both for commissioned work and one-off shots submitted speculatively. Some magazines pay handsomely and promptly, while others seem to think that photographers should be grateful just to have their picture published with a credit alongside.

The latter magazines seem to thrive more on their contributors' goodwill than on any sound business footing, expecting writers and photographers to fill up their pages for next to no financial reward. If they have enough readers who will oblige with words and pictures, then they feel they have no need to spend money on professional talent or pay photographers more than a nominal fee.

Money isn't everything, of course, and there are occasions when even the best-paid photographers are happy to give their pictures or their time without payment: to a deserving charity or cause, for example. But magazines that operate in the commercial market-place should pay commercial rates to their freelancers. If an editor tries to fob you off with a derisory payment, make sure you cross him off your Christmas card list and give his magazine a wide berth in future.

Some magazines (well respected and influential, but with small circulations) are regarded as a prestige showcase for a photographer's work. A portfolio in one of these magazines may be viewed as good publicity, even though fees are small. Such exposure can be beneficial, especially for a photographic newcomer.

A one-off sale of pictures to a magazine is good; an on-going relationship is better. This is why the personal approach is important. If you remain just a name at the bottom of a letter, then there is little incentive for an editor to phone you up and offer work. Let him put a face to the name and get to know you a little.

Many magazines have an informal group of freelance writers and photographers on whom they can regularly call to produce copy — people whose professionalism the editor respects. These freelancers may not be asked to contribute to every issue, but the editor will know their individual strengths and will offer them work that suits their styles and personality. If you can build such a working relationship, then you have the chance of regular work.

Once you have worked for a magazine it's really up to you to keep the trail warm. Keep the editor informed regularly that you are alive and well and available for work. Suggest new ideas well in advance of the publishing date. A phone call, however brief, keeps your name and specialities in an editor's mind.

When contacting magazines start with the ones you already read; you will be acquainted with their usual style and content. Buy copies of other magazines with which you are less familiar. Remember that any magazine or periodical can be ordered via your local newsagent; the shop will almost certainly have a list of all the magazines currently being published. The *Writers' and Artists' Yearbook* also lists magazines, and gives some advice about potential for freelance contributions and, in some instances, the usual fees paid.

Photo-Press

The photographic press provides an almost tailor-made outlet for photography. The professional photographic journals offer few opportunities, however, since their picture allocation will generally be taken up with the work of established professionals and news-based features. Short portfolio sets — perhaps only one per issue — provide precious little space for highlighting new photography.

The hobbyist magazines, on the other hand, have a rapacious appetite for uncommissioned pictures. Full-blown portfolios will come from a variety of sources, and very few of them will have been commissioned; photo magazine budgets just don't run to that kind of expense. They are interested, instead, in seeing existing work, and a good portfolio from a rank unknown will have every chance of being accepted.

It's no more than sour grapes to suggest that your pictures won't be wanted because you are not a household name, and rejection of your work is likely to reflect nothing more than the quality of your pictures. The big names of photography do attract readers, of course, but the photographic magazines realise that running page after page of slick and sophisticated pictures — using models, equipment and locations that few amateurs could afford — is likely to repel more readers than are attracted.

So the photo magazines usually like to run pictures that hobbyists can identify with: pictures that illustrate a particular technique or way of seeing. Subject matter is actually less important than providing a purely *photographic* interest, to inspire and inform readers who are eager to use their expensive bits of matt-black hardware to more creative effect.

The weekly photographic titles run innumerable features dealing with fairly elementary photographic techniques. There are many hardy perennials, such as the use of filters in colour and in black and white photography, with 'before and after' pictures that illustrate the effects that filters can produce. Concepts that flummox every new crop of photographic novices need explaining: depth of field, panning techniques, choice of film for various purposes and lighting levels, simple processing and darkroom procedures, etc.

The same topics crop up again and again, often on a yearly cycle, because there is always a healthy crop of new readers being attracted, while others switch to one of the more upmarket monthly magazines. Spring is the time that the hobbyist's camera is taken down from on top of the wardrobe and dusted off; the magazines will major on outdoor photography and related techniques. Autumn is the time they try and persuade their readers to get down to some serious darkroom work, so articles focus on processing and printing practice.

Every season, too, has its more general features, offering ideas to those photographers who have more equipment than imagination. Summer brings a rash of features: shooting beach scenes, traction-engine rallies, sporting occasions and other events that drive the camera-toting public out of doors in great numbers. The first week of November seldom goes by without a colourful article on shooting firework displays; nor will the January issues often be without advice on photographing snowy landscapes.

This cycle gives the freelance photographer plenty of opportunities to see his work in print, provided he submits seasonal material well in advance of the appropriate publication date. Accepted pictures are likely to be used to illustrate points which arise from the text, so it's important to supply captions giving the relevant information, such as make of camera, lens, film, filters (if used), as well as subject, location and any photographic trickery involved.

Shooting Covers

Magazine work — whether speculative or commissioned — offers many options in the way that pictures are used. It's the job of a magazine designer to juggle the pictures and typeset text to give the most pleasing arrangement on a page. Strong photographs can be emblazoned across a double-page spread, or a picture story may be built up by a number of smaller pictures in sequence.

Every magazine has it's own 'house style' — in the choice of things like typefaces, headlines, choice and use of photographs, etc. Good design can give a magazine its own distinctive character — an increasingly important matter when the bookstands are so crowded with titles.

Thoughtful design no doubt helps a magazine to sell, but there's one aspect over which editors, designers and publishers agonise endlessly: the cover. Editors know that the majority of their readers are 'regulars' — people who will buy all or most of the issues. But there is also a pool of 'floating voters' who can be seduced into making an impulse buy when confronted by an eye-catching magazine cover.

Many topics and interests, such as gardening or DIY, are covered by a wide variety of periodicals. Buying one or another may similarly depend on nothing more complex than seeing an attractive cover picture. The difference between a good and bad cover may literally be represented by thousands of readers won or lost, which is why so much effort is expended to make sure that the magazine package is as visually exciting as possible.

Shooting cover pictures for magazines is a demanding business — for a host of reasons — requiring disciplines that apply to few other kinds of editorial photography. A cover picture has to be an arresting image in its own right, technically and aesthetically top-notch. It has to fit the magazine's format: typically a vertical A4 paper size. Around the subject of the picture there should be room to add text: the magazine's own name (the 'logo') at the top, and abbreviated listings of the issue's contents (called 'tasters' or 'cover lines') elsewhere on the cover.

Cover pictures need to be bold and colourful; subtlety has to take a back seat in terms of immediate impact. Primary colours are more popular with editors than muted pastel shades, and simplicity will win every time over a complicated or fussy composition.

Now then, how many pictures in your portfolio meet all these criteria? Very few, I'd bet, and probably none at all. Your carefully composed and tightly cropped transparencies may be well suited to most editorial purposes, but are unlikely to produce effective magazine covers.

It's for this reason that the choice of cover pictures is a never-ending headache for editors, one that occupies a disproportionate amount of time. Those photographers who can produce suitable images will make regular sales, and many editors will pay handsomely for pictures that will profitably enhance their products. One or two hints will increase your chances of acceptance . . .

Which Format?

Although 35mm is acceptable for the inside pages of all but a handful of magazines, old habits die hard when editors are looking for cover shots. The problem is not only the size of an image: the shape is important too. The dimensions of a 35mm transparency are actually quite similar to an A4 magazine cover. For a 'full-bleed' cover (ie one that runs to the edge of the paper on all sides) the transparency will be reproduced very slightly larger than A4, and then trimmed down to size. This will reduce the usable size of a 35mm slide. A further slice must come off top (or bottom) to compensate for the slight discrepancy between the shape of a 35mm frame and an A4 cover.

A magazine's logo may occupy as much as the top third of the cover, and the principal subject of a picture should not normally encroach into this area. It can be seen that these necessary croppings leave little room on a 35mm transparency for the subject itself, which is why larger film formats tend to be better received. Many editors insist on roll-film transparencies; 5 × 4in images will be more welcome still.

Bigger transparencies offer finer definition, a greater choice of croppings and a more substantial canvas on which the magazine designer can work. After all, he has to trace the picture onto a mock-

up of the cover, and incorporate all the textual information that will later whet a potential reader's appetite when the magazine is picked up from the news-stand.

This mock-up (called a layout) will provide detailed and complex instructions to the colour originators: specialists who will transform all these ingredients into the final glossy result. It's at this stage that a few tricks of the trade can help transform a suitable image into a stunning cover. The predominant colours in a picture can, for example, be echoed in the colours of the tasters, logo, or background. If a transparency doesn't quite fit the cover format, then a uniform background colour can be 'extended', by careful retouching, to the edges of the cover. Pictures can be laid over headings, and vice versa. A skilled retoucher can work wonders, but only if he is given a suitable transparency in the first place. And that's the photographer's responsibility.

A bleed cover is the natural choice, giving the magazine maximum impact on the shelf. There are times, however, when a 'boxed' picture is preferred, ie one which is confined within a square or rectangle, and which does not bleed to the edges of the cover. A boxed image may be part of a magazine's house style, or the chosen transparency may simply not stretch to the full dimensions of the cover. The boxed format can even allow a rectangular picture to be used horizontally, or for a number of pictures to be printed side by side.

While it is possible for any kind of picture to grace a cover (and even black and white images occasionally get the nod), this does not negate the need to shoot covers with full-bleed treatment firmly in mind.

A picture like this—though in colour, of course— could be a candidate for a magazine cover, perhaps a countryside publication, or one devoted to a particular county. The dimensions would suit a 'full bleed' cover: ie one which occupies the entire cover area. There is ample room to include a large magazine logo at the top, without destroying the picture composition; space, too, for the 'tasters'—abbreviated listings of the features appearing in the issue.

Editors take immense pains to choose the most appropriate cover pictures for their magazines, since an attractive image may help to attract many new readers: 'floating voters' who want a magazine on some specific topic, but who are not regular readers of one title. Few pictures take naturally to being plastered with multicoloured text and design features, while still retaining some visual integrity. Photographers who can shoot pictures with cover potential will get a positive response from editors.

Photographers who shoot magazine covers regularly tend to produce more shots than would appear to be necessary. But if you have taken the trouble to visit a particular location, or hire a model and studio, then it makes sense to come away from the shoot with a set of pictures that give a magazine designer as many options as possible in the way the images could be cropped.

Keep the pictures simple and graphic. The subject should be colourful without being garish; a composition that relies on the interplay between just two or three colours is ideal. Ensure that nothing detracts from the image's impact. Space at the top of the picture should be left as blank as possible, to allow the magazine's logo to be dropped in. When doing a studio shot this blank area may be a roll of coloured background paper; in a landscape it might be uncluttered sky or sea. Other areas of plain colour, either side of your subject, will allow the tasters to be printed — often in a contrasting colour for maximum visibility.

Study the covers of magazines over a period. Recognise the house style: bleed or boxed images? Size and position of logo and tasters? Is the style restrained or frantic? Which subjects seem to be preferred? Are they shot 'straight', or is a degree of photographic trickery in evidence? Clue into the needs of editors and designers and you may have the chance to see your pictures prominently displayed in the newsagents. But be warned; shooting successful magazine covers isn't as easy as it looks!

Insight: Barry Hunter

Barry Hunter is the editor of *SLR Photography* magazine, a publication that will be familiar to many readers. His wide experience of the photographic press includes stints on *Practical Photography* and *Creative Photography*. He has also worked as a freelance writer and photographer. He has, therefore, plenty of interesting comments to make about the way magazines are produced, and the opportunities available to freelance contributors.

'*SLR Photography* has a tradition of reader involvement, so we are pitched between the technique magazines and those which mainly feature portfolios of photographers' work. We actively encourage photographers to send in their pictures, whether they be just a few favourite shots that we can hold on file for possible use or an illustrated article. We use both readers' pictures and stock shots from picture libraries, in an effort to make the magazine as accessible as possible to the targeted readership.

'We want pace and variety in every issue: variety of subject matter and approaches in the photography and in the styles of writing. In a scale of importance we rate the photographs top, followed by captions, headings and then the main text of the feature. It's all about making the pages look good. After all, people will read the magazine cover to cover once they have bought it, but it's the pictures that will make them choose initially between one photographic magazine and another.

'We are always on the lookout for individual shots of outstanding quality that will make good covers. They don't have to be glamour shots. We do cover glamour photography inside the magazine from time to time, but we try to treat it just like any other subject. There's no doubt, however, that the right sort of girl picture can identify an issue as a photographic magazine. The picture just has to be different from the kinds of shots you find on either men's or women's magazines. It could be a head-and-shoulders portrait of a girl, with an element of eye-contact, but it must have some photographic input.

'Whenever possible we like to tie in the cover picture with one of the features or portfolios inside the magazine. This helps the reader to find his way around the magazine. It's got to be an outstanding shot, though, and if there's nothing suitable from within the features then we usually have to go to a picture library. So there is scope for freelancers to drop suitable images onto my desk. We plan to use full-bleed cover pictures almost exclusively, to give continuity from issue to issue, so photographers should think about how we would be able to accommodate the logos and tasters.

'Inside the magazine we have three or four regular features, in which we use readers' pictures. We are keen to get pictures that we can hold in our files; it's convenient for us to use these pictures to illustrate all kinds of photographic techniques. We have a large file of black and white prints, and now we are particularly keen to see good colour transparencies. We can't make any firm promises that the pictures we file will ever be published, so we appreciate that many freelancers will not want us to hold onto their work in this way.

'It's different when people send in work as a possible portfolio; we try to give photographers a firm yes or no as quickly as possible. And if we say yes, then they will definitely be used. If the answer is no, then we try to return the work promptly so the photographers concerned can submit them to another magazine. We will often suggest a magazine that might be interested in their pictures. Sometimes, of course, we need prompting to make a decision, since so much work arrives in our offices each week. The "100 per cent" pictures go straight to the top of the pile and will probably appear in the next issue, while the "20 per cent" pictures get sent straight back. It's the in-between work — the "60 per cent" shots — that are difficult to make a decision on.

'All the photographic magazines are in the same field, and yet they have very different requirements. Editors spend a great deal of time analysing their magazine's particular position in that market. We see that the appeal of *SLR Photography* is basically to advanced amateurs: people who band themselves into clubs and who want some reaction to their work. They've taken the straight record shots and now they're looking to shoot more creative pictures. So the pictures we use are one step removed from the most obvious inter-pretations, taken by photographers who really think about what they are doing. On the other hand, if you use pictures that are *too*

A shaft of sunlight breaks through the clouds and illuminates a pair of fishing boats on a millpond of a sea; the scene looks too perfect to be true. And that's because the picture has been assembled in the darkroom from three separate negatives: the main sky image plus the two boats transferred onto lith film. Careful applications of Farmer's Reducer accentuated the sunbeam and the light reflected off the water. The purist might look askance at such darkroom manipulations, but *all* photography is a two-dimensional representation of a three-dimensional reality. To a point it's all artifice.

The amateur photographic press are avid users of pictures which illustrate photographic techniques: everything from the use of special effects filters to more advanced darkroom trickery. Submitted pictures need detailed captions on how the particular effects were accomplished; if the captions can be extended into a short article then so much the better. (Photograph: Derek Sayer) sophisticated, then the readers won't be able to identify with them. They won't be able to relate the pictures they see in the magazine to the pictures they take themselves. In a mainstream magazine you need to keep a balance between what looks good on a page and what will be accessible to our readers.

'We take a lot of care with the captions that appear alongside the photographs. I'm tired of seeing uninformative captions in photographic magazines. A caption is more than a label; it can really set the scene for a shot. So we like to see captions that are as comprehensive as possible. The more details that a photographer supplies, the easier it is for someone on the magazine to write a caption that says something about a technique and then relates it to the particular photograph. And it should go without saying that all pictures submitted should bear the photographer's name and address.

The Written Word

'We have quite a generous budget for features, so we are interested in seeing illustrated articles. However, it's always advisable to check whether the proposed subject would be suitable. After all, there are at any one time a couple of issues of the magazine in the pipeline which the readers haven't yet seen. They won't be aware of what you have planned. So a phone call to an editor could save a lot of fruitless work. He will be able to offer some constructive advice, even if he can't use the feature in his own magazine or is already planning to use a similar idea in a forthcoming issue.

'There is a hard core of freelancers who understand how magazines operate. They'll see changes in editorial policy, and will submit features and pictures that will fit the new requirements. The better a freelance gets to know an editor, the more he'll be able to target his work successfully. You'll know their stuff is good, so you'll use them regularly. So there really are opportunities on *SLR Photography* for those photographers and writers who are willing to look closely at the style and content of the magazine.'

Local Press

There are literally hundreds of local newspapers around the country. Some are major publications with a large staff and extensive circulations, while others are almost one-man operations filled mainly with parochial news about weddings and flower shows. There are dailies, weeklies and the ubiquitous 'free sheets' which in many areas are threatening the viability of 'paid-for' newspapers.

The sheer proliferation of local newspapers might seem to offer good opportunities for part-time freelance photographers, but it's important to understand how they operate. Daily newspapers cannot afford to rely on casual freelance photographers. News 'goes cold' very rapidly, so staff photographers will be assigned to cover local events; they will also respond to the hard news stories which naturally cannot be anticipated.

Picture editors maintain a diary of events, enabling them to assign jobs to the staff photographers on a day-to-day basis. Typically these jobs will comprise hard news pictures, 'soft' news such as local events, weddings and politics, sport and features.

If you look through your local paper you will notice that 'people pictures' predominate; the name of the game is human interest. Celebrities present outsize cheques to local charities, men in suits shake hands to publicise a business merger, members of clubs and organisations line up for the camera. Local news revolves around local people; it's as simple as that.

Many local papers are actually quite light on pictorial content. A large percentage of the pictures appear to be printed for no other reason than to sell glossy prints to the participants.

So what are the opportunities for freelance photographers? Given that staffers are dispatched to cover major local stories, there are basically just two ways for a freelance to see his pictures in print.

The local press occupies much editorial space in covering events within their immediate area. There is always scope for freelance photographers to play their part, if they contact the editor beforehand. If there is too much for the often over-stretched staff photographers to deal with, then reliable freelancers may get the nod. In most situations it is the photographer's responsibility to supply fulsome captions to his pictures; people pictured enjoying themselves need to be identified.

In this shot — taken at Alnwick's annual medieval fair — the people enjoying themselves are mostly behind the photographer. During the fair, any misbehaviour (real or imaginary) is punished by the 'miscreant' being ducked into a deep pool of water: all good clean fun — for the onlookers!

Firstly, he may be able to offer a one-off photograph of a news event that happened too quickly for staff photographers to capture the scene. A blazing building, a road accident, a 'bit of aggro' following a football match: pictures of events such as these may interest the editor of your local paper, provided the negatives can be delivered with enough speed to meet daily deadlines.

Secondly, a freelance may be able to take up the slack when staff photographers are busy, or at times (weekends and evenings) when they are not available. Since these are the times when part-timers *want* to work, there may be regular work for freelancers who can be contacted by phone whenever a suitable job arises.

Those who are keen to work for a local paper should contact a member of staff: the picture editor (if there is one) or the editor. A phone call is all that's needed to discover whether or not the paper has spare capacity for freelance photographers. If the response is positive, the editor will want to see your portfolio with a few examples of recent work.

Human Interest

Whenever you show your portfolio you should try to tailor the pictures to that particular market. To get work from local papers you ought to angle your selection towards people: portraits, candids, famous faces, people attending events, etc. You won't impress the editor with your landscapes or wildlife pictures, however good they may be.

If the editor likes the look of your pictures, and is convinced that you will be able to handle local assignments quickly and efficiently, you may get regular work. It may not be very exciting, unless photographing the attendants at a dinner-dance or presentation is your idea of excitement! It will certainly not be very well paid, though reasonable expenses can generally be claimed. And you may find that you will be called out at short notice, which can play havoc with your social life . . .

Photography is seldom a matter of overwhelming importance on local papers, and the pictures used are mostly uninspiring 'mug-shots', group portraits and heavy-handed efforts at a little visual humour. You will have to produce much of the same; your 'creative' interpretations are unlikely to impress!

The low budgets that local papers earmark for photography make such work unrewarding. Since you won't get rich you'll probably have to settle for getting a credit line when your pictures are used and a few tear-sheets for your portfolio.

National Papers

Provincial newspapers have one major advantage for the freelance photographer or writer: no matter where you live there will be a paper published in your immediate locality. National papers, however, huddle unapologetically in the capital. They used to be lumped under the catch-all title of 'Fleet Street', though recent moves to dockland sites have made this term as redundant as the picketing printers. The changes — and the spectre of new technology — have revolutionised the newspaper industry, though they may leave photographers in other parts of the country quite unmoved.

The nationals tend to take photography more seriously than the provincial papers, in the knowledge that an exclusive picture story may pull in a few thousand extra readers: a vital consideration in such a competitive business. The nationals field large teams of staff photographers, covering both 'hard' and 'soft' news stories. They will be kept busy on a great number of assignments, only a few of which will ever appear in print. Some papers have regional offices, but most of the staff photographers will be London-based. Some stories can be foreseen, so that photographers can be dispatched in good time; but the nature of many news events makes it impractical for staff photographers to cover them and still meet print deadlines.

This is where out-of-town photographers can contribute. All the larger towns around the country boast news agencies, and their own staff photographers will tackle local stories. The resulting pictures will then be offered to the national papers (and for syndication) on a regular basis. These sources — the staff photographers of the papers themselves and the local agencies — supply the lion's share of the pictures you see when you leaf through the national daily and Sunday papers.

So what's left for the independent freelance? There may be

News photography often requires a good deal of courage. In theory the photographer is regarded as a neutral observer; in practice, however, he may have to operate with people who react aggressively to the idea of being photographed. The death of a freelance photographer during the city riots a couple of years ago has made many photographers think twice about their own safety when involved in potentially violent situations.

This shot of an arrest during a demonstration is typical of the kind of news picture that a freelance has regularly to take. More important than composition is *being there:* getting into the thick of the action to give a graphic representation of a newsworthy event. The deadlines for daily newspapers require great speed — not only in shooting pictures, but also in delivering films to the papers' darkrooms. (Photograph: Russell Boyce/Anglia Press Agency)

opportunities to act as a 'stringer', ie covering picture stories in your own area. But you will need to be available at short notice if you hope to get regular work. The ability to drop everything and respond to a phone call is vitally important.

The only use for yesterday's news is to wrap fish and chips, so the news photographer always has to work at a canter. Stories must be covered, and films processed and printed, at a speed that hobbyist photographers would find bewildering. The papers are in competition with each other, and in the circulation war the first paper to run a major news picture will gain perhaps many thousands of extra readers.

Scoops

It's up to the photographer to ensure that a scoop picture arrives at the picture editor's desk as quickly as possible. So what do you do if you think you have a unique or unrepeatable shot of an event that is bound to hit the headlines? In such a circumstance (admittedly not one you will experience very often) don't waste time in the darkroom. Instead, make a phone call to the newspaper that you think would be most interested in your picture, and ask for the picture desk. Alternatively, contact a local press or news agency. Give details about your potential scoop; you will be told whether or not you are likely to have a valuable commodity to sell.

If you get the thumbs-up, and you happen to be a London-based photographer, you will probably be able to deliver your film in person and negotiate a fee while the pictures are processed and printed. Those photographers outside London will have to make other arrangements. British Rail's Red Star parcel service offers speedy delivery by train — at least from major provincial railway stations.

Many press agencies have a wiring service: an ingenious way of sending prints down the phone line. Agencies may also be able to syndicate your photographs, thus providing greater profits from your 'exclusive'. In any case, news agencies will have greater experience in the matter of negotiating fees, and stories of inexperienced photographers signing away their rights to exclusive news pictures are legion: shots which later went on to make a great deal of money, but not, unfortunately, for the photographers concerned.

Picture Libraries

Many freelance photographers like to market their own work, dealing directly with clients. The benefits of the 'do-it-yourself' approach are obvious, in that the ensuing profits don't have to be shared with any middlemen.

The trouble is that few photographers are as adept at marketing as they are proficient with a camera. Many photographers appear before the bankruptcy courts each year and the cause is nearly always a lack of business acumen rather than any creative shortcomings. It takes time, energy and aptitude to sell yourself and your work in such a competitive field as photography, and it's all too easy to find yourself becoming more of an accountant and salesman than a photographer.

There's a lot to be said for letting a third party market your work, while you concentrate on what you know best: the making and taking of images. One option is to join forces with a representative: a specialist who makes a living by drumming up assignments for a small number of photographers. This is essentially a personal service which is realistically open only to established professionals, and the agent's job is generally to generate new commissions rather than to sell existing work.

This is unlikely to be an option to most readers of this book, yet the marketing 'muscle' and expertise of an agent need not be denied to the part-time freelance. Picture libraries are important inter- mediaries in the business of visual communication. And it's very big business indeed.

To understand the role of a picture library we have to acquaint ourselves with the methods used by publishers to find the photographs they need. They can hire a photographer, and brief him to cover specific topics on their behalf. This can prove an expensive option. A publisher who needs a photograph of the New

York skyline at dusk is not likely to pay a photographer to jet across the Atlantic just to get this one shot in the can. It can also be an impossible option. If a publisher wants pictures of, say, wintry landscapes in high summer — quite likely, considering the forward planning that many branches of publishing need — then there is no possibility of shooting the pictures in time.

This is where stock photography has an important role. Since just about everything on this planet has already been photographed many times, publishers may be able to find many of the pictures they need in files of existing work. But where do they look?

It's the responsibility of picture researchers to trawl all the sources of existing photography, on behalf of publishing clients, to find suitable images. These sources include the files of individual photographers, archives and specialist collections of pictures — plus picture libraries whose holdings are continually being increased and upgraded by working photographers.

Picture researchers will usually have a list of pictures to locate. These wants might be general, such as a shot of a palm-fringed beach or a busy street thronged with shoppers. Alternatively, the subject might as specific as 'Ayrton Senna taking a right-hand bend during the 1985 Monte Carlo Grand Prix' or 'aerial view of Stonehenge'. Tracking such shots down is a demanding job that's made a little easier due to the existence of picture libraries.

Stock Options

Libraries come in all shapes and sizes. Some are simply the stock pictures of a single photographer; others are huge companies with

It's the most natural thing in the world to photograph children, and good photographs of children — from birth to adolescence — are perennial sellers. It's equally natural for photographers to begin with their own children, though parental feelings should be kept in abeyance if good pictures are to result. Standard family portraits of kids grinning or grimacing at the camera have next to no sales potential; their place is in the family album.

Children may have a short span of attention, but this can help the photographer; it shouldn't take long for children to ignore the presence of a camera, and become absorbed in some activity. This 'grabbed' shot was possible simply because the photographer was carrying a camera on a family outing. The symbolism of a child running down a path is something that won't be lost on a picture editor. A picture like this could illustrate a child's early feelings of adventure and independence, as well as being a pleasingly simple composition.

offices all round the globe and hundreds of 'name' photographers on their books. Some market pictures — for a cut of the profits — on behalf of their photographers, while others prefer to buy pictures outright. A fairly comprehensive listing of libraries can be found in the *Writers' and Artists' Yearbook*.

Libraries exist primarily as intermediaries between clients and photographers. Their strength lies in detailed knowledge of the markets and ability to negotiate the most favourable rates. The photographers on their books will find that their pictures are being circulated daily to a wider range of potential clients than any one photographer could ever hope to contact. Library staff have their fingers firmly on the pulse of commercial photography; their work enables them to keep abreast of new trends and tastes in visual imagery. These changes can be relayed directly to the photographers so that they continue to shoot marketable pictures.

Most picture libraries will handle every aspect of the marketing process, leaving photographers to busy themselves shooting saleable stock photos. So far so good; the sting is that for their services a library will charge a healthy commission — commonly 50 per cent of the negotiated fees. This seems, at first sight, to be disproportionately high. Why should any photographer lodge his best pictures with a library, when the profits are split down the middle?

The answer lies in the marketing ability of a good library. It exists to offer pictures to a wide range of potential clients, and will have the kind of 'inside knowledge' of these markets that most photographers will lack. The library will naturally respond to requests for particular images from its clients, but will also be actively involved in developing new markets and contacts.

This marketing exercise isn't cheap and a library's overheads are likely to be large. It takes a great deal of work to service the vast communications industry with a constant supply of still images. The fifty-fifty split of sales fees provides a strong incentive for the library to work hard on behalf of the photographers represented. And the photographers may well discover that 50 per cent of regular picture sales is much better than 100 per cent of precious little!

Keeping Copyright

Some libraries prefer to buy photographs outright, but photographers should think long and hard before signing away their copyright for a flat fee. Most, however, are in the business of *leasing* photographs: selling the right to publish pictures rather than the pictures themselves. This means that pictures can earn an income for both photographer and library over a period of perhaps many years.

In most cases a library will undertake every task associated with picture sales, from cataloguing photographs right up to sending out photographers' cheques. The process of getting newly acquired images onto the desks of picture editors and researchers takes some time; this is why many libraries stipulate a minimum period of time for holding a photographer's inventory of pictures. This is commonly three or five years.

Some photographers may find this an unreasonable stipulation, but there are sound reasons for it. A library will put a great deal of effort into promoting a photographer's work; that work will be in vain if the photographer decides he wants his pictures returned after a few months. Photographs may be duplicated for wide distribution, and they may appear in the library's catalogues and promotional material. These are important sales tools and it can be mildly embarrassing for a library to admit that pictures reproduced in a catalogue are not actually available.

It may take years to exploit the sales potential of a photographer's best pictures, so it's to everyone's benefit for the photographer to view his relationship with a picture library as a long-term project. If nothing else, the rather rigid-sounding 'rules' serve to discourage time-wasters. Photographs lodged with a library should be 'written off' as far as the photographer is concerned; he should let the library get on with the job of marketing them as profitably as possible. Pictures which a photographer might want back in a hurry should not be submitted to a library at all.

Another condition which some picture libraries insist on is an exclusive contract; ie an assurance that the photographer will deal with no other libraries. Reputable libraries take great care not to sell an image to competing clients. This is to avoid, say, two magazines sporting an identical picture on their covers in the same month, or having a photograph cropping up in two different advertising campaigns. It does happen, but fortunately not often. It may be the library's fault, which will do its reputation no favours. If a photographer sells a picture identical, or similar, to a shot already lodged by him in a library, then it's *his* fault.

Which Library?

It can be seen that a photographer must make some serious decisions before approaching a picture library. Is he willing to place what may be a large inventory of photographs into someone else's hands for a period of perhaps five years? Does he have sufficient confidence in the library's ability to exploit the full sales potential of his work? Would he be better off marketing pictures himself? And which library, after all that, will offer the most fruitful relationship?

A glance through the *Writers' and Artists' Yearbook* will reveal that photo libraries have their different specialities and ways of operating. Some collections and archives are complete in the sense that no new submissions or photographers are required. Others are really the picture files of one or two photographers who are content to market only their own work. The libraries we are concerned with here are those actively looking for fresh submissions of top-class photography.

Some libraries cater for very specialised markets and their wants are tailored accordingly; they may deal only in sporting pictures, for example, or botanical subjects. Others provide coverage of a particular country or district. A photographer whose output coincides with the needs of a small, specialist library may develop good sales in equally specialised markets.

The non-specialist photographer will be better advised to approach a larger library: one dealing with international clients in advertising, packaging, promotional and editorial markets. His pictures may form only a very tiny percentage of the library's picture stock, but they will probably be offered to a greater number of potential clients. It's a debatable point whether it's better to be a big fish in a little pond, or a little fish in a big pond.

Some libraries won't look at a small submission of pictures; they want photographers on their books who will continue to submit pictures in volume, and are not really interested in photographers who have just a dozen stunning pictures. Other outfits are

There are potential sales through picture libraries for photographs dealing with almost every subject and photographic style. But the kind of photographs that will see *repeated* sales are generic—that is, they manage to sum up, in one frame, a particular place, time, person, event, etc. This shot of downtown Las Vegas seems to represent the American love affair with the internal combustion engine.

What makes the shot stand out from similar pictures is the quality of light; it makes the road glisten like a river of gold and picks out the telephone wires. The low light, and the use of a telephoto lens, has made a simple and dramatic picture that, in different light, might have been a rather cluttered composition. (Photograph: Malc Birkitt)

interested in quality rather than quantity and will accommodate good photographers with a more modest output of pictures. Again, a minimum submission of, say, 500 images has a lot to do with discouraging time-wasters and photographers who are not serious about stock photography.

Once you have found a library that appears to fit the bill, you should write (with stamped addressed envelope) for confirmation that it is interested in taking on new photographers. If the answer is yes then it's up to you to prepare a submission of stunning transparencies . . .

The Need for Colour

Most libraries concentrate solely, or primarily, on colour transparencies. It's easy for a photographer to market his own black and white images. With negatives stored safely at home, he can print and distribute his photographs at will. If a print goes astray, or is damaged, then he's lost nothing more than a sheet of printing paper and a few minutes of his time.

It's one of the ironies of commercial photography that the prices paid for colour images are far greater than for black and white. It doesn't bear any real relationship to the effort that a photographer puts into his work; but that's the way it is. Colour transparencies, unlike black and white prints, are irreplaceable. They are also vulnerable to being lost or damaged. Even a tiny scratch from careless handling can render a transparency worthless, since the scratch will be greatly magnified when the transparency is enlarged for reproduction.

It's a sad truth that not everyone handles transparencies with the same care as the photographer, and once they have embarked on the perilous journey towards final reproduction they pass through many hands. They are perhaps most prone to damage while actually being scanned by a colour originator, since they will be without mounts or other protection during the process.

The problems are great for a picture library with an inventory of perhaps a million images. A single transparency won't make repeated sales around the world, because it can only be made available to a single client at any one time. The answer lies with duping: the precision copying of transparencies to provide any number of direct duplicates.

Duping transparencies is no easy task; done badly it can kill the impact of the strongest images. Done well, however, it can offer results that are virtually indetectable from the originals. Unlikely as it sounds, duping can even *enhance* the originals, by modifying any colour casts and giving a closer crop. The costs of duplicating transparencies may be met by the library alone, or shared with the photographer. It's a comforting thought to realise that your pictures are being seen by clients all over the world, in the form of duplicates.

The prices realised by picture libraries vary according to the uses to which the photographs are put. Advertising clients will generally pay better than editorial, and a picture that's destined for a major advertising campaign on the nation's hoardings will naturally attract a bigger fee than it would as an illustration to accompany a magazine article. The stock photographer can leave the business side to the library, and get on with shooting film.

Mutual Trust

Since his photographs are, hopefully, being marketed so widely, how can the photographer be sure that he is actually being paid for every picture the library places with clients? Well, he can't, but libraries thrive on goodwill, as well as contacts. Most libraries conduct their business with scrupulous honesty; the market is too profitable for a library to risk its hard-won reputation.

However, the novice's burning desire to have his pictures published has spawned one or two phoney agencies which require photographers to pay a signing-on fee. A worthwhile agency will thrive on their commission alone; be very wary of agencies that want *you* to pay *them*.

They may sound convincing, and even offer more attractive rates, such as a better split for the photographer than the usual fifty-fifty. You may find that they make their money from photographers' signing-on fees rather than from picture sales. And have nothing to do with agencies that promise to sell your pictures for you while they are still in your own files. Don't fall for 'get rich quick' advertising copy; reputable libraries seldom need to advertise their services in the amateur photographic press.

If a library accepts *all* the pictures you submit (with or without a signing-on fee) then you have further grounds for suspicion. Either you are a photographic genius or the library has ulterior motives. Decide for yourself which is the more likely scenario!

Shooting Stock Pictures

Picture libraries service every possible market in which photography is used, and a general, non-specialist library will be interested in virtually every subject that can be photographed. The more comprehensive a library's inventory of pictures, the more likely it is that clients will be able to find the exact pictures they are looking for. A library will, after all, soon gain a poor reputation if it promises much but can seldom deliver.

A great number of the pictures we see every day will have come from picture libraries, ie they will have been picked from collections of existing photography instead of being specially commissioned. Picture credits, where they appear, will offer further clues. For editorial uses, at least, library pictures generally bear the name of the photographer and the agency which represents him: for example, *Joe Bloggs/Picture Source*. If you really scrutinise these pictures you will soon begin to understand what stock photography is all about. The photographs you see are successful shots; they have sold.

Shooting stock is halfway between commissioned work and personal photography. To some extent it's the photographer's responsibility to shoot the pictures that he believes will be saleable, though most libraries are happy to keep both new and established photographers informed about current picture requirements. Many libraries issue up-to-date 'wants' lists, detailing subjects both general and specific; these can be very helpful in pointing photographers in the right direction.

This sort of feedback is very important for photographers, who might otherwise be working 'in the dark'. It's to the benefit of both photographer and library that picture submissions fit the library's collection of pictures and extend its scope. Matters of style, cropping and format can be discussed with a member of the library's staff. It's always a good idea, when first considering shooting stock, to visit a library in person. The photographer will be able to see some of the library's inventory of pictures and get a good understanding of the working methods and cataloguing systems. A library will give as much guidance as possible to talented photographers, but the latter should not expect to be continually spoon-fed with advice. Stock photography requires them to come up with a continuing supply of self-generated picture ideas.

Picture libraries catalogue their pictures with great care, to make it easier for particular images to be found for clients. Subjects may be logged on filing cards, with cross-indexing for pictures that might be grouped under more than one subject heading. Some of the larger libraries now have their catalogues and records on computer, and even pictures transferred to videodisc, so that a client making a personal visit to the library will be able to enter his picture requirements on a keyboard. A few seconds later he can scroll through suitable images on a screen and view them at his own pace. His choices will then be found in the files, so that he can leave the building with the relevant transparencies. Such high-tech facilities will no doubt become commonplace in the years to come.

This ease of viewing means that stock pictures need to stand out strongly at first sight if they are to attract repeated sales. For the most part, pictures sell on merit alone; this is one market which does not necessarily favour famous names. It's for this reason that a talented photographer doesn't need wide experience of commercial photography to shoot stock successfully. And he doesn't have to work full-time. But he *does* need to develop an understanding of how to shoot the kind of pictures that a library needs for its many clients.

High Standards

It would be hard to overestimate the need for top-quality imagery. Those photographers who make a living from stock photography do so because they take the business very seriously and practise the sort of quality control that most manufacturers would envy. The truth is that picture libraries are not dumping grounds for second-rate transparencies. Those photographers who find their dealings with picture libraries unrewarding are generally those who submit a motley pot-pourri of reject slides for which they can't find any better use. And a library which accepts substandard transparencies is one that any proficient photographer should avoid.

Stock pictures go through at least three editing procedures. The photographer himself should whittle down his output into a submission of the highest quality. A member of a picture library's staff—well versed in the matter of picture selection—will reduce the numbers further. If pictures are unlikely to sell, then the library won't want to clog up their files with 'dead wood'. Then, and most importantly, pictures will be vetted by potential clients. They may have less visual awareness than either photographer or library staff, but they do control the budgets available for buying pictures. And in stock library terms a good picture is one that attracts the greatest number of sales.

Clients will often have to view pictures very quickly when making their choice. Similarly, the pictures they choose will need to have an immediate appeal to the final link in the chain: the magazine reader, the book buyer and the consumer who must be persuaded by advertising to buy one product rather than another. In the world of fine-art photography, the viewer may give a picture in an exhibition or monograph many minutes of his undivided attention. But in most commercial markets pictures have to be assimilated more rapidly.

So a good stock picture is one which presents one mood or one item of visual information in a way that immediately captures the viewer's attention. Since just about every subject has sales potential in one market or another, *how* you take a picture is as important as *what* you take.

It's a good rule to keep things simple. A clear, uncluttered image will get its message across more effectively than one which is tricksy or over-ambitious. Unfussy backgrounds allow the principal subject to stand out unambiguously; the viewer won't give the picture a second glance if the subject isn't immediately apparent. Give great attention to detail: a catch-light in the eyes of a portrait subject, or an unrevealing facial expression, can make the difference between a saleable picture and one that misses the mark.

There is another reason for shooting simple, graphic images whenever possible. The most successful stock pictures are those which sell repeatedly in a variety of markets. It is common for pictures to be cropped for reproduction to a different format from the one the photographer envisaged. And pictures are often combined with text, headlines or superimposed design features to produce what the designer considers to be a lively visual impact.

Composition

It's drilled into most photographers to produce tightly composed images, though for many purposes a looser composition will provide the end-user with more options. Although 35mm film is too small to allow more than a sliver of the transparency to be lost, roll-film (especially 6 × 6cm) is more adaptable. Few pictures are reproduced square, so sales are more likely from pictures which can be cropped in both vertical and horizontal formats without losing any important elements of the picture.

In formats that give rectangular images it's natural to shoot predominantly horizontal images; most cameras, especially 35mm, handle better than when held vertically. So picture libraries are always looking for good vertical pictures. This is especially relevant for shots that might have the potential to be used on magazine or book covers.

Clear backgrounds or areas of uniform colour need not be a waste of film; they can be a godsend to picture buyers. Sky, sea, sand, deep shadows, studio backdrops and green foliage are examples of backgrounds which offer the client a variety of options in the way a picture might be used. Clear space at the top of a picture (especially a vertical shot) allows text or logos to be conveniently 'dropped in'. A uniform colour gives further opportunities for words to be picked out in a harmonising or contrasting colour for maximum visibility.

Remember that stock pictures are not end-products; they are tools of the communications business. Clients buy reproduction rights for pictures that meet their individual needs. You may not like the idea that your pictures will be emblazoned with advertising copy, crowned with a magazine logo or cropped in a way you hadn't envisaged. But you have to accept this treatment, and shoot pictures that facilitate the work of all the publishing specialists: picture researchers, art directors, editors, designers and printers.

Insight: Will Curwen

Will Curwen is a photographer from Liverpool who spends much of his time shooting stock pictures for a major picture library. Years spent on location work in the States and Canada have given him a self-reliance to match the technical and creative excellence that successful stock photography demands. His advice on the subject should help to enlighten those photographers who have the mistaken impression that stock photography is an easy option.

'The most important consideration is to find a good picture library. There are a great number of libraries and they all operate in slightly different ways — covering different areas of the market. If you're a still life photographer, for example, then it's no good putting your work into an agency which is orientated towards people pictures.

'The best approach is probably to write to an agency with a selection of, say, twenty of your best transparencies mounted in a plastic filing sheet. In your covering letter you can enquire about the library's particular specialities, the kind of clients they have and the kind of marketing they do — whether they syndicate pictures overseas or deal with the UK only. A lot of libraries have booklets which offer useful guidelines to photographers.

'If the library shows interest in your work, then you can arrange to meet the picture editor with your full inventory of slides. Check out how tidy the library is; a tidy library is likely to be a good library. If you see pictures lying around in cardboard boxes gathering dust, then you might realise that it's unlikely to be a very efficient operation.

'Find out, too, what film format the library prefers: 35mm is quite acceptable for the editorial market but if you want to sell your work for greetings cards and calendars then you'll need to use roll-film or larger. Many of the people who buy pictures from libraries are not visually literate and find it easier to view larger transparencies on a light-box.

'If your pictures are of a rather specialised nature — such as sport or natural history — then you may find it more profitable to deal with a small picture library that handles your kind of work. Your pictures might get rather lost in a big library that holds millions of general images.

'Edit your pictures thoroughly and submit only your very best work; it's better to show 200 good photographs than 2,000 mediocre ones. You should keep in close contact with the picture editors so you begin to understand what kind of pictures to shoot. It's not easy to work out what the current trends are, and a style which is currently out of fashion may well come back into vogue next year.

'Once you have pictures lodged with an agency don't worry if they don't start to sell immediately; it takes time for pictures to be edited, catalogued and put into circulation. Once your pictures are selling, a good library will give you a monthly or quarterly sales report. This will give details of which shots have sold, who bought them, how they have been used and for how much money. By studying this information you can gain a valuable insight into the commercial market, and refine the pictures you take so that they become more saleable.

'I spent a lot of time with the US picture editor from my photo library, finding out exactly what kind of pictures he wanted. It was time well spent. Stock pictures have to be technically superb and capable of being reproduced using both the crudest and most sophisticated of methods. They also have to relate to the cultural values of the market area you've chosen.

'In the USA, for example, they like deeply saturated colours and a strong graphic design, and the overall feel of the pictures should be cheerful. In Britain, at present, there's a strong bias towards escapism in popular culture, especially advertising. So the images that sell well over here are romantic and evocative.

'More abstract compositions will sell in Europe. For example, a picture of a row of trees along a skyline, with a field of yellow rapeseed flowers and a blue sky, will sell and sell in Europe. But not in the States . . .

Looking to the Future

'I try to take pictures which will last as long as the film emulsion itself will last; so I'm looking ten, twenty, thirty years ahead. I'm concerned, in my pictures, with a sense of universality; they must have a very direct appeal to human nature. This is a tremendous challenge — to become not merely a camera operator but a cultural iconographer, creating images that help people to understand the world they live in.

'I've spent a good deal of time studying how films are made: how they actually respond to colour and light. If you shoot 35mm then there's a distinct market preference for Kodachrome. It's easy to reproduce and enlarge; it's archivally stable and convenient to make duplicates from. Kodak have been refining the film for fifty years now, and I reckon they've got it right; optically it is tailored to the visual response of the human eye.

'Fujichrome has also become very popular, so I've done comparison tests with both films on the same subject. Kodak gives a totally convincing illusion; it looks "real". But with Fujichrome — good as it is — you know it's a fantasy rendition of the colours that you see.

'Yet all films have their particular fortes. When you get hazy conditions in summer, for example, it can be difficult to filter out the ultraviolet light with Kodachrome. You can sometimes end up with a magenta cast. Fujichrome cuts through the haze like magic while Ektachrome tends to give bluish results, especially on overcast days. Most of my landscape pictures are taken when the sun is thirty degrees or lower in the sky; in these circumstances Kodachrome comes into its own.

'For roll-film or sheet film most picture libraries prefer Ektachrome or Fujichrome. The roll-film version of Kodachrome is a very exciting new development; it will revolutionise the stock picture industry.

'It's important to keep a neutral or slightly warm colour balance in most of your pictures. Libraries are not keen to accept pictures that have a cold feeling. This is particularly true of the skin tones in people pictures.

Filters

'There is a great variety of special-effects filters you can use, and there's been a vogue for screwing as many filters as possible in front of the camera lens, in an attempt to make a silk purse out of a sow's ear. They have to be used with great care since it's difficult to make filtered shots look convincing. For example, some of the cheap graduated filters can make a picture look like a nuclear bomb has gone off! If you're determined to use filters, then make sure you buy

It's difficult to quantify just what makes one stock picture sell and sell, while another shot will languish unsold in a picture library's files. But it's a wise stock photographer who regularly checks which of his images are making consistent sales, and who tries to analyse just what makes these shots so successful. This will help him to keep new submissions of pictures as commercial as possible.

A stock photographer cannot afford to be self-indulgent; it's to unseen clients (and not himself) that his pictures must appeal directly. His pictures must speak eloquently for themselves, since the photographer will not be around to influence most clients' decisions. Stock pictures tend to sell on visual impact alone; the reputation of the photographer is of comparatively little importance. (Photograph: Will Curwen) the best. The same applies to camera equipment; you don't need a lot of lenses to shoot stock successfully. Just buy the best you can afford, since technically poor or unsharp pictures are never going to sell.

'When you are out taking pictures, keep your finger off the shutter. You don't *have* to take the picture. If you dilute your creativity by taking hundreds of mediocre pictures just to get one good one, then you are simply wasting time, money and film. But if something good is happening in front of you then I see no point in taking one picture and walking away.

'When I feel a picture is right I might shoot as many as a dozen frames — changing the composition to provide both vertical and horizontal croppings. This will give a picture buyer the choice when it comes to working out page layouts. Shoot some of the versions with patches of clear sky or an uncluttered foreground, so that they could be reproduced along with superimposed headings or text.

'Once you have a certain number of pictures lodged in a library it's important to keep making regular submissions of photographs: perhaps once every couple of months. Apart from increasing your earnings the library will know that you are committed to shooting new work. But edit out all but your very best shots; ask yourself the question "Is this picture valuable enough for someone to pay good money for it?" The days are gone when photographers could off-load their reject pictures into a photo library.

'There are a lot of dedicated amateurs (I mean amateurs in the true sense of the word: people who take pictures for the love of it) who could do well in conjunction with a good library. When you shoot stock you are fairly anonymous; generally speaking it's not your name or reputation that sells pictures. If your pictures are good enough then there is every chance that they will sell again and again.'

Entering Competitions

Competitions can be an excellent way of dipping your toe into the turbulent waters of commercial photography, to see if your pictures pass muster when judged against the other entries. And if you're going to take the time and trouble to enter competitions, then you might as well aim to win.

Photographic competitions are everywhere. The specialist photographic magazines, naturally enough, run them almost incessantly. They serve a variety of purposes. They encourage 'reader participation': an important factor for any magazine. Manufacturers of photographic equipment are more than happy to put cameras and accessories up as prizes, in return for a healthy blurb about their products when announcing the competition and, later, to accompany the results. This publicity — outside the advertising pages — is always welcomed by manufacturers.

The magazine readers benefit from this largesse by having the opportunity to upgrade their equipment with new products and materials; even foreign holidays are offered occasionally as prizes. Everyone likes competitions, it seems, except the unfortunate person who lands the job of parcelling up and returning the pile of unsuccessful entries . . .

But photographic magazines represent only the tip of the competition iceberg. Since most people own cameras, and have an over-inflated concept of their photographic abilities, it isn't hard to persuade them to enter competitions which have genuinely worthwhile prizes. General interest magazines run them from time to time, with themes generally linked to their own particular subjects. A tie-in with an appropriate product manufacturer or supplier will ensure that prizes are good enough to ensure a healthy response from readers, and enable the magazine to run the contest at little cost to themselves.

Women's magazines, for example, will commonly ask for baby and child photographs in their competitions; sporting publications may look no further than their own speciality to attract entrants. Almost every kind of photography will be catered for by the competitions that are run every year.

Most competitions are genuine: that is, the prizes are worth winning, the rules are fair and winners will be chosen on photographic merit alone. So competitions offer excellent opportunities for photographers to shoot on specific themes, edit their own work and choose the best shots to enter — good training for any kind of commercial photography.

Those photographers who are members of camera clubs will already know a thing or two about the competitive aspect of photography. Clubs seem to delight in organising print criticism sessions, 'slide battles' and inter-club contests, generally with trophies as prizes rather than money or equipment.

The trouble with club competitions is their 'traditional' nature; judging criteria can often be little different from what they were a century ago. A dogmatic approach to composition, the 'rule of thirds', and conventionally photogenic subjects can make a rather rigid framework for assessing photography. The best aspect of club competitions is that they require members to edit their best pictures and present them in a visually attractive way: a useful discipline to develop in every branch of photography.

Illustrating a Theme

Having found a competition that you want to enter, there are a number of matters to consider before you drop your potential prize-winners in the post. All photographic competitions will specify a

A torrent of 'white water' and a determined canoeist make a combination that can bring out the best in the action photographer. This print has won a number of awards for the photographer in club competitions, and it's not hard to see why. The canoe itself may be hidden, but the raised paddle and the man's expression leave us in no doubt about the excitement of the moment. The rush of water adds to the picture's impact, and directly involves the viewer.

Photographic competitions can provide a useful incentive to a potential freelancer, since they require him to shoot pictures on assignment, edit his work dispassionately, print to exhibition standard and finish off the job by spotting prints, matting and mounting. (Photograph: Mick Rouse)

theme, and a surprising number of entrants are disqualified simply by sending pictures that don't illustrate the theme.

Your first thought may be to wade through your picture files in search of one or more appropriate images to enter. You *may* find something eminently suitable; it's actually more likely that you won't. Whatever the theme happens to be, the judges will be on the lookout for imaginative interpretations.

A theme like 'Water-sports', for example, will elicit hundreds of near-identical windsurfing or yachting shots, which will bring an involuntary yawn to the most enthusiastic of judges. Most shots will look — correctly — like they've been dragged from the photographers' files. The judges will invariably respond favourably to entries which appear to have been shot specifically for their competition. These occasions offer the nearest thing to a commercial brief that many hobbyist photographers will ever get: a genuine opportunity to dream up interesting picture ideas and transfer those ideas into finished images.

Take the given theme (we'll stick with 'Water-sports' as a typical example) and jot down your more imaginative ideas as they come to you. If some of the ideas offer unusual — or perhaps humorous — interpretations of the theme, then so much the better. Ideas that excite *you* may well have a similar effect on the judges.

The water-sports theme will naturally conjure up conventional activities, such as sailing and canoeing. No matter where you live there will be a club not far away, and a phone call to the club secretary will probably furnish you with dates and venues of races and outings. Few people will object to being photographed; some will be happy to help you to get the shots you want.

Active participation in sailing or canoeing events may produce stimulating pictures: instead of shooting from a distance with a telephoto lens you may be able to persuade a canoeist to come close enough to your waterside vantage to allow the use of a wide-angle lens. The immediacy of white water and swirling paddles is likely to produce more exciting results than 'sniping' from afar. Effective photography often demands that you put yourself out, not merely taking the easiest option. A little originality will pay dividends, no matter what kind of assignment you're working on.

The close-up idea could be taken a step further. An underwater housing for your camera, for example, could allow you to go right into the surf and spray without worries about damaging your equipment. You might have to hire such a watertight housing by the day, but then you could defray the cost by shooting stock pictures at the same time.

The water-sports theme might ring some less obvious bells. Cricketers may head for the pavilion at the first hint of drizzle, but many other sportsmen regard rain as just one more natural hazard of their chosen pastime. Soccer, rugby—even bowls—require more than rain to stop play, so there will be many opportunities to photograph sportsmen and women as they compete against the weather and each other. Spectators huddling beneath their umbrellas might complete the scene.

Children have their own brands of water-sports. Puddles and small children seem to attract one another like magnets; uninhibited play might provide opportunities for off-beat pictures. These suggestions show merely that there are many ways of interpreting a given theme, and that a little thought and pre-planning can often produce successful pictures.

Reading the Rules

Competitions are always announced with a fanfare, with details of the prizes to the fore. The small print will be buried in the less prominent rules of the competition; these should be read carefully and understood. There are likely to be a number of restrictions and stipulations about entries, all of which have to be observed.

Some competitions are for amateur photographers only; this is generally understood to mean people who earn no more than 10 per cent of their income from photography. There will be details about the number and format of acceptable entries. If colour slides only are acceptable, then there is no point in sending prints. If the maximum size of prints is laid down as 10 × 8in, then don't print any larger. Stick to the requested number of images. The rules are generally clear and simple; nevertheless, a percentage of entrants will always disqualify themselves by not reading them.

It's a general requirement that each submitted image should bear the photographer's name and address. The judges will have to separate the better pictures from the also-rans in order to whittle the entry down to the final winners. If all pictures are suitably tagged with the photographer's details then there should be no problem in returning them after the competition is over.

A stamped addressed envelope is often required for this purpose; don't expect to see your pictures again if you forget this simple task. Disclaimers by the competition organisers about loss or damage to entries should not cause any qualms. Such disclaimers are standard for all situations in which photographs are sent by post; be assured that all reasonable care will be taken with your entries.

Competitions provide excellent opportunities for photographers to tackle a given theme with skill and imagination. The skill covers such aspects as composition, focus, correct exposure and print quality, but it's *ideas* that finally sort out the wheat from the chaff when competition judges are sorting out their shortlists. Most entrants will provide obvious interpretations: the hackneyed viewpoint and the easiest option. Prize-winners, on the other hand, will have taken the trouble to treat the competition as an assignment — instead of just pulling a few shots out of their picture files.

This shot, showing a severe example of modern architecture, has won the industrial and commercial section in one of Ilford's annual Photographic Awards. (Photograph: John Russell)

Quality Counts

Having complied with these rules you can get down to business: choosing those pictures which will catch the judges' eyes. No matter that some names appear with monotonous regularity as prize-winners; most competitions are judged with scrupulous fairness, considering that personal preferences are bound to play a part.

Technical excellence is paramount, as always. Check for critical focus, correct exposure, print quality, etc. Obvious technical short-comings will not endear the judges to your pictures, however good they may be in other respects.

A single image will be a stunner — naturally — while a selection of photographs should provide a strong thematic link. Remember that your pictures will be competing against a great many others, so make sure your submission makes an immediate and positive impression on the judges.

It is useful to understand how competitions are judged. A typical competition will attract, say, a thousand entries. All will be viewed; after all, it is to the benefit of everyone connected with the competition that the strongest pictures pick up the prizes. But that first viewing will be undertaken at some speed, to weed out obvious non-starters. These will comprise at least 90 per cent of the total entry, leaving fifty to a hundred entries to go through to the next stage. This is likely to be the point at which a 'celebrity judge' (if there is to be one) will peruse the entries.

It's not too hard to ensure that your entries go into that 10 percent pile, since a dispiriting number of the rejects will be badly printed enprints, with precious little photographic merit.

The pile of 'possibles' will become ever smaller as pictures are scrutinised ever more closely. Transparencies will probably be viewed *en masse* — on a light-box rather than being projected. Experienced picture editors will be accustomed to viewing even 35mm slides in this way, with the aid of a magnifying loupe. Prints will be laid out on tables, so that the judges can stroll around them and work slowly towards a final choice.

This is where images will be compared directly with one another, and the finer points discussed. Which pictures have illustrated the given theme most effectively? Which of them shine out with that indefinable 'something' that makes the judges nod in appreciation? Will the most imaginative entries stand the magnification that reproduction will entail? It can be a long, though often pleasant, task to choose the eventual winners; it's up to you to ensure that your pictures are among them.

Prizes are generally donated by manufacturers, who are happy to offer equipment in return for free publicity before, during and after the competition. This publicity machine may involve prize-winners being invited to an award ceremony; photographs of the prize-giving may be used in press releases and news features. There is little point in asking for cash in lieu of a prize; what you do with it subsequently is, of course, entirely up to you.

A Note of Caution

This chapter began with an assurance that most competitions are run in good faith. Most . . . but not all. There are some which reputable photographers should avoid. Copyright of entries should remain with the photographers concerned; don't enter any competitions that entail handing over copyright to the competition organisers. A photograph good enough to win a major competition could eventually earn the photographer thousands of pounds; don't swap that earning potential for a one-off prize.

Apart from the actual winners there will be other entries which the organisers might want to use for their own publicity purposes. They should always pay reproduction rights for this privilege, and copyright should *always* stay with the photographer.

Be wary, too, of competition rules which say that no entries will be returned. You can, of course, always make another print from a negative, but transparencies are irreplaceable. Restrictive rules of this kind give competitions a bad name. It is common practice, on the other hand, for entrants to pay for the return of their work, and for competition organisers to hold onto submissions until such payment is forthcoming. Unclaimed entries will generally be thrown away after a few weeks.

It can be seen that some competitions are nothing more than excuses for generating inexpensive photography. A recent competition in a men's magazine actually offered prizes that were less generous than the standard payment for acceptable glamour photography. Don't be taken in: read every competition rule carefully and decide whether the enterprise is worth your time and trouble to enter.

Insight: Mick Rouse

Mick Rouse is a paste-up artist by trade, and a photographer by inclination. As a leading light of the Peterborough Photographic Society he has used his experience in club contests to become a regular winner of national photographic competitions. The highlight of this secondary career was taking first place in a major competition organised by Kodak last year. With cars as the theme Mick entered two evocative prints of a vintage Austin, and scooped — to the understandable envy of his friends — a brand new Porsche sports car.

Mick's first success was nearly ten years ago. Since then he has won a variety of prizes: trophies, cameras, lenses and projectors, as well as cash. Less talented photographers might consider him lucky, but Mick points out — quite rightly — that luck plays only a very minor role in winning competitions.

'The first prize I ever won was a camera, and there was a prize-giving ceremony at the Savoy Hotel in London. That success was a springboard for me; it seemed great to win a camera just by putting a slide in the post! I began to think about competitions in a more "professional" way, by improving the quality of my entries.

'Over the years I have built up quite a large collection of slides. So when a competition was announced I would go through them to see if any shots would fit the bill. More often than not, however, I would think about producing work specifically for a competition.

'The first step is to read and re-read the competition rules. There is no point in sending a stunning shot if it doesn't abide by the rules. If the rules suggest a maximum size for prints, it's no good sending anything larger. If three pictures comprise an entry, don't submit four. Then I study the theme of the competition, trying to discover what kind of pictures the judges want to see. Sometimes you have to read between the lines.

The picture that won a Porsche coupé for photographer Mick Rouse: it shows an Austin Eton car shot on Kodak's Infra-red film. Mick decided that the film's unique characteristics suited this particular subject. Infra-red film makes green foliage glow a snowy white, darkens a clear blue sky and lightens clouds. The results can often make a picture appear to have been lit by moonlight. In this case it certainly made the eyes of the competition judges light up.

Mick's success in photographic competitions relies on developing an eye for the unusual subject or viewpoint, good photographic technique and a willingness to put a great deal of effort into every entry. He tries to place himself in the judges' shoes, and to read between the lines of the competition rules. A little thought on behalf of the photographer will ensure that his competition entries at least reach the judges' shortlist. (Photograph: Mick Rouse)

'Many competitions invite entries that illustrate a single theme. One, organised by a battery manufacturer, was 'energy'. The first thing I do is look up the word in the dictionary, to give myself preliminary ideas. Under "energy" there was electrical energy, kinetic energy, water energy, etc. I get flashes of inspiration, but I've also got a bad memory, so I try to jot down picture ideas as soon as they occur to me.

'I know that many people will send in shots that are very obvious, so I always try to produce pictures that will stand out from the crowd. That can take a lot of research and planning, such as hiring models and costumes. You may need to invest quite a bit of money, film and time to get the results you want.

'For example, I entered a competition organised by a fertiliser company, which was sponsoring a national village cricket knockout ending with a final at Lord's. The plan was to publish a calendar, and photographers were invited to submit pictures for it which had been shot at any of the preliminary matches. The brief was to epitomise the essence of village cricket, so I knew the judges wouldn't necessarily be looking for action shots.

'So I did a little research. I found out where matches within reasonable driving distance were due to be played. Then I phoned the sports editors of local papers to find out what the grounds were like. I discovered that one of the grounds, near Kettering, was in a meadow and surrounded by trees. It sounded perfect.

'I drove there on the day of the match. Luckily it happened to be a beautiful summer's afternoon. On the boundary there was a huge checked table-cloth, set out for a picnic. I used this as the foreground for one shot, with the cricketers in the background. Another was a telephoto shot of a dog being waved off the pitch by one of the players. In all I took about seven rolls of film: black and white and colour on both 35mm and 6 × 45cm equipment. I entered the maximum number of pictures — six — and these two shots were used on the calendar, winning me £250 each.

The Good Old Days

'The Kodak competition was run to coincide with the launch of a new range of black and white printing papers. The theme was "cars" so I knew a lot of entries would feature gleaming paintwork and chrome. But Kodak's papers seemed to be harking back to the "good old days" of fibre-based printing, even though they were all new products. So I thought I'd also go back to the good old days for my pictures . . .

'A friend of mine has a collection of vintage cars, including a beautiful old Austin Eton. I wanted to shoot it on Kodak's infra-red film; it has a lovely ethereal quality which can give a nostalgic effect. To exploit the film's unique characteristics I needed a sunny day with a clear blue sky and contrasty light. One Sunday we got what we wanted, so we drove around some local villages photographing the car against old stone houses.

'I printed up two of the shots onto Kodak Elite paper. It took me twenty sheets to get the prints I wanted; I couldn't see much point in entering a Kodak competition with second-rate prints. Some people have said that the winning print is boring — that's fine — but I just say that it's brought me a Porsche . . .

'Sometimes, however, you can be too clever for your own good, entering pictures which appeal to *you* more than they are likely to appeal to the judges. For example, I've never managed to win any of the competitions run in women's magazines. There always seem to be thousands of snapshots entered, and one of them always seems to get first prize. You may send in some sophisticated picture which won't get a second glance. The judges may simply not be looking for "professional" quality, as you can see when you look at the results.

'One competition in a women's magazine offered a holiday in Spain as a prize. The winning picture was of two children digging on a beach with their buckets and spades. Another competition had an all-expenses-paid holiday for four, and the winner was . . . two children digging on a beach with their buckets and spades. The second prize was an airline bag; guess who won that!

'The last thing to remember about competitions is the importance of presentation. I generally mount my slides in black card masks. The judges can simply drop the card onto a light-box or hold them up to a window. Entries are almost never projected; the judges know what they are looking for and if they need to check for sharpness they will use a magnifying loupe. When I make prints I ensure they are of exhibition quality. Good presentation won't make you a winner but it *will* get your pictures noticed. If picture captions are requested I will type them on a separate sheet of paper, including technical details such as camera, lens, film, special effects used (if any), shutter speed and aperture.

'When I see an interesting competition advertised I cut the page out of the magazine, and keep the pages together in order of competition closing dates. In this way I can always give myself enough time to shoot pictures for each competition I want to enter. I don't enter competitions unless I feel I have a realistic chance of winning; I feel that would be just a waste of time.

'On the other hand, it's no good looking at the results of a competition and thinking "I could have done better than that . . ." The first rule about competitions is that you can't win if you don't enter!'

SHOOTING FOR SALES

The Subjects to Shoot

It is a major step from shooting pictures as a pleasurable hobby to shooting pictures for possible publication, though the two aspects are by no means mutually incompatible. Photographs should be taken for a purpose, whether to fill the family album, build up a portfolio or submit to a publication. The subjects you photograph, and the way you photograph them, are vital considerations.

For example, windsurfing has blossomed in recent years as a popular participation sport, and a number of magazines have been launched to give the avid windsurfer something to occupy his mind when the wind stops and his local gravel pit is as calm as a mill-pond. There is a corresponding demand for good windsurfing pictures to grace the magazine pages.

If you turn those pages, however, you will see that a great number of the pictures will have been taken overseas. Those glorious breakers, deep blue skies, sun-tanned bodies and elaborate windsurfing stunts seem to be a long way from our own beaches — which, in most cases, they are. Your pictures of a sporty chum pottering round the local estuary beneath grey clouds don't really have much sales potential, since more exciting and evocative pictures will be arriving daily at editorial offices and picture libraries.

It's a shame to waste time, energy and film on unproductive assignments, when a slight change in approach may be all that's needed to produce pictures that sell. There are very few subjects that will not sell, as you will find when you leaf through some of the 'pictures wanted' lists that some of the picture libraries issue. You will find subjects listed which you almost certainly had never considered shooting. Here are a few wants taken at random from one such list: Modern factory and warehouse exteriors. Heathrow Airport, terminal 4. Banks — interiors and close-ups of customer/

Saleable photographs of children don't need to feature only smiles and grins. A picture such as this could illustrate some childhood fear or trauma — accentuated by the direct gaze, uncertain positioning of the hand and the plaster on the finger. In fact, the pictures that precede and follow this shot show him playing up happily for the camera. This picture seems to capture a moment of private reflection, or is it just mere role-playing? Either way it's the result that counts.

While you are unlikely to run into problems when publishing candid portraits, you should be aware that an inappropriate caption can transform an innocuous picture into an unwarranted slur on the subject's character. Children — other than your own — should be approached via their parents, since your photographic efforts might otherwise be misinterpreted. The signing of a model release form by the parents will be a further safeguard.

cashier transactions. Man using car telephone. Aftermath of burglary. University graduation day (caps and gowns, etc). Theatre audience from stage. Discotheques. Factory production lines. Modern drawing office interior. Family barbeque. Black or Asian people in modern work situations. Crowds. Pigeon racing. Passing baton in relay race. Henley Regatta. Water droplets on painted surface. Rows of new cars awaiting delivery. Petrol tanker off-loading at garage (pump prices not to be seen as this dates the picture). Free-range chickens. Door of number 10 Downing Street with policeman.

These subjects—taken from a list of over 200—are, in most cases, very specific. You might think they are also rather mundane, but somebody out there wants them enough to pay good money for them. If you think carefully about them you may be able to deduce what uses these pictures will have — whether for magazines, trade journals, books, advertising, promotion, postcards, calendars, chocolate-box lids, etc. Some of these pictures can be found by simple observation; others can be set up. All can be taken with a little planning and forethought.

This section deals with a variety of subjects in turn, offering hints as to how they may best be approached. There are no hard and fast rules about shooting saleable pictures, except that the photographer should have an end-use firmly in mind before he takes each picture.

Personal Style

There is always room for a personal style, as photography is never the objective recording medium that some people imagine. Your own tastes and vision should not be abandoned for bland uniformity. The suggestions that follow are intended merely as a guide, so that the part-time photographer can begin to recognise those events and moments which offer most potential.

Styles change in every creative activity, whether it be architecture, music or graphic design. Creative solutions which are in demand one year may simply be outmoded twelve months later. Photography, too, has certain trends and fads, and it is important for all photographers to be aware of them.

For example, the 'inspirational' photographs of the sixties can look rather naïve in the hard edged eighties, and soft-focus pictures of a couple walking hand-in-hand along a sunset beach may be viewed by picture buyers as a tired old cliché. Not that photographic clichés don't sell: just make sure that you are producing today's clichés rather than yesterday's. Better yet, find your own contemporary way of viewing your surroundings, and let that be reflected in your photography.

Like groceries, photographs have a 'shelf life': a period during which they will have a value to picture buyers. In the case of a hard news picture that period may be only a matter of hours, while a

A hazy summer's afternoon with low sun, a sparkle on the water and the picture elements deliberately registered by the photographer as virtual silhouettes. There is seldom just one 'correct' way of exposing a picture; it's the photographer's responsibility to pre-visualise each scene and try to recreate that vision on film, using any photographic techniques that are appropriate. He may go for maximum visual information or, as here, sacrifice detail to emphasise the prevailing mood.

landscape shot without any features that might date it could be selling for many years. A straightforward record of everyday life in the eighties may hold little interest today, but will become a valuable piece of evidence to the archivists of the next century.

This time element is an important consideration, especially when shooting stock photographs in the hope of making repeat sales over years rather than months. There are many factors that will date a picture, such as changing fashions in clothes, cars and architecture. The purpose envisaged for each picture should influence what details are included and what are left out. Truly 'timeless' pictures

Some pictures communicate by giving the viewer visual information. Others, such as this tranquil seascape, offer mood and atmosphere. Such images engage the emotions rather than the intellect, and effective mood pictures are sought by a wide variety of publishing markets: advertising, packaging, posters, editorial, etc. Human nature being what it is, however, the demand is greatest for 'upbeat' pictures which conjure up pleasant associations.

Evening light on water does just that: the gently soporific effect of waves lapping against the shore. The silhouetted figure occupies only a tiny portion of the picture area, yet is a vital element in the composition. The photograph makes us wish we'd been on this beach at this particular moment; we can't ask more from a mood picture than that. (Photograph: Colin Leftley)

are rare (even the landscape undergoes changes) but a carefully selected viewpoint and composition can ensure that stock pictures don't date too quickly.

There are many subjects which need careful study by a photographer if his pictures are going to sell successfully in his chosen market. Whatever subjects are chosen you can be sure that other photographers are tackling them too. And many of them will be experts on their subjects as well as proficient with a camera.

It's difficult, for example, to shoot nature pictures without an abiding interest in wildlife. The naturalist-photographer will have the knowledge and patience to get pictures that reveal as much as possible about the animals, plants and landscapes that he photographs. He will have a good understanding of animal behaviour and their life cycles. He will be able to provide comprehensive and intelligent captions to each picture. He has a great advantage over the photographer who sees the subject as just one more topic on which to train his camera.

In the early stages of building a portfolio and developing photographic skills there's a lot to be said for sticking to what we know best. Involvement with a subject will naturally show up in the pictures.

People

'People pics' are a photographic staple, like rice in Chinese cookery. It's natural to photograph people; the majority of camera owners shoot little else. And what better subject is there than the people we love: family and friends enjoying themselves on holiday and special occasions? But there is much to learn, and unlearn, about photographing people if picture sales are to ensue.

'Human interest' pictures attract buyers and readers, as every editor and advertising executive well knows. We instinctively identify and empathise with people in photographs. The drought-ravaged landscape of Ethiopia, when seen in a photograph, may influence our thoughts about Third World economics; but it's only when we see a starving child in that bleak landscape that we are truly *moved*.

Images of war emerge from our TV sets in a flickering frieze. Bombs drop, bullets whine and we watch in fascination. But then we see the face of an exhausted soldier, eyes blank from seeing too much conflict, and we begin to *feel* the futility of war.

People at work and play offer endless opportunities for the photographer — from candid shots to formal portraiture, character studies to glamour. But for those accustomed to photographing within the family circle it can be quite traumatic to train a camera on total strangers, whether shooting candidly or setting up a portrait session.

Candid photography captures people as they are, and not necessarily as they would see themselves. There are a number of ways to photograph people without their becoming aware of the photographer. The obvious way is to shoot from a distance with a telephoto lens. This will normally isolate faces and features against a more-or less blurred background, but says next to nothing about a person's relationship with his environment. Worse, it's sniping with a camera; the subject almost becomes a quarry, being stalked by a hunter with a loaded camera. When your hapless subject meets your eyes along a 300mm lens you will feel, correctly, that you are snooping.

You can actually be less of an intrusion if you move in close, and use a standard or wide-angle lens. Many reportage photographers consider the 35mm lens as their 'standard', ie that best equates with the way they see with the unaided eye. This approach requires an involvement that will be reflected in the pictures; the viewer will feel almost part of the action, and not an objective observer.

A wide-angle lens gives such a broad view that many people will not be aware you are photographing *them*, especially if they appear towards the edge of the viewfinder image. Practised reportage photographers can raise a camera to their eye, focus, check the exposure and shoot — all in such a smooth motion that their actions go unobserved. With a wide-angle lens fitted, the focus also can be pre-set to, say, ten feet, giving a good depth of focus for most street photography. The camera can be brought up to eye level or even fired 'from the hip'.

This kind of fly-on-the-wall social-documentary photography may work as single images: people in their environment, going about their daily business. Or they may work as a series, documenting a culture, an event or a place. A series of photographs on a particular theme may become a picture story, with the addition of text and captions, while single pictures of people have many illustrative uses.

Sales Potential

Almost any human activity will have sales potential in one market or another, but the photographer needs to have a firm idea of the pictures he wants to take. Little is generally achieved by wandering the streets at random, waiting for pictures to happen.

Saleable stock pictures may be found in any situation — urban or rural — for photographers with a little imagination. Trades and professions, for example, could inspire a host of picture ideas. Rural locations could feature farmers at work — sowing, ploughing, harvesting and haymaking. Farming practices change, and these changes can be reflected in pictures. Stubble-burning is a contentious issue in many parts of the country, and whenever the subject crops up in print there is a good chance that an appropriate picture may be needed to add visual emphasis to the words. Hundreds of publishable pictures could be taken on a single farm, so varied are the tasks that farmers have to do.

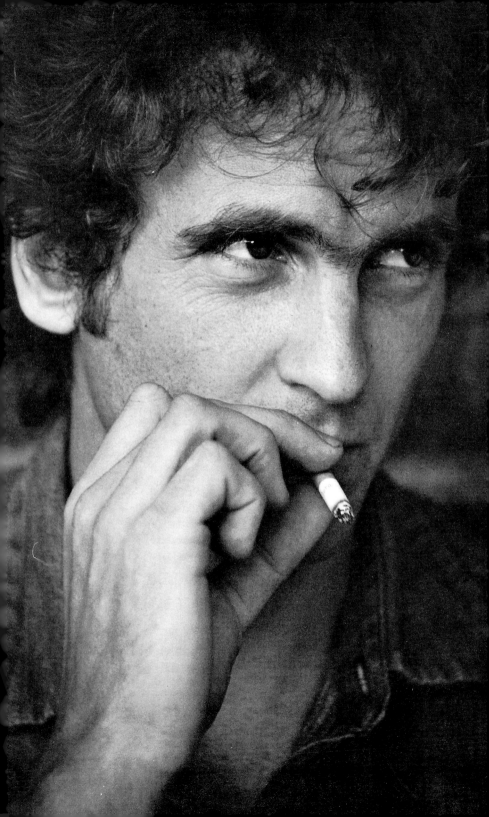

The cities change too; areas are demolished and new buildings built at a startling rate. Show people at work on these projects and you may get saleable shots, particularly via a suitable picture library. Scaffolding and bulldozers may make interesting pictures in their own right, but workmen will add human scale and interest.

Candid pictures of people at work or leisure need not reveal very much about their character or personality; for many illustrative purposes it may even be preferable for faces to be hidden, since candid photography precludes the signing of a model release by the subjects.

There is a constant demand for 'situation' pictures of people by every kind of publication. A magazine picked at random from the news-stand will prove the point. But candid photography implies that the photographer does not stage-manage the scene in the viewfinder: pictures are 'taken', not 'made'. There are many occasions when the photographer needs the active participation of his subjects.

It's not surprising that some people object to being photographed informally, since a camera can be very intrusive. People in the public eye accept being followed by a posse of photographers, but the rest of us may be unhappy to find ourselves under such scrutiny. But a direct approach by the photographer may make the subject more co-operative, if you explain your reasons for taking pictures.

Set-up pictures range from asking a total stranger if he will mind you photographing him, to the hiring of models to create a totally pre-planned picture. Situation pictures, whether candid or set up, are not really portraits; the people pictured are representative of a *group* of people. An illustrative picture of, for example, a farmer busy stubble-burning, is saying more about farming practices than

Portraiture does not require elaborate studio set-ups; natural light can be very effective, especially if it is diffused and doesn't cast harsh shadows. If the quality of the light is contrasty the shadows can be 'opened up' with fill-in flash or a makeshift reflector. Non-directional illumination is ideal. That may be no more difficult to find than an overcast sky, which acts, after all, as a giant diffuser to filter the sunlight. Direct sunlight seldom flatters, since it makes people screw up their eyes.

This is a grabbed shot, taken only with soft light from an adjacent window. A necessarily small aperture provided little depth of field, but the blurred background and tight cropping help to draw the attention to the subject's eyes and intense gaze.

about the individual you have chosen to photograph. But the picture would be much less interesting if that element of human interest were to be excluded.

Portraiture is a different matter, and one which requires a rapport, however brief, between photographer and subject. The photographer concentrates on his subject's individual characteristics, and hopes to bring out some of his personality through a suitable choice of pose. Clothes, facial features and bodily attitudes give visual clues to the viewer, but it's up to the photographer to plumb a little deeper into the sitter's character and then reveal this extra dimension in his photographs.

Characterful portraiture is a difficult discipline, and many photographers are unable to tackle it successfully. Nervousness in the photographer can easily be transferred to the sitter, whereas a confident air and a ready wit will help to put the sitter at ease.

The techniques and psychology of portraiture need a whole book to themselves, and there are many useful guides to the subject. Suffice it to say here that it's to the eyes in a portrait that the viewer's own eyes naturally go. Much of a person's personality is revealed in the eyes, so ensure that they are in crisp focus.

Famous Faces

Newspaper photographers spend much of their time photographing the faces of the famous (and sometimes infamous). Political and showbiz events are accompanied by press photographers packed shoulder-to-shoulder, getting shots for the morning editions. Photocalls are public-relations exercises that allow photographers access to newsworthy subjects in a controlled environment.

Few of these opportunities will be open to the part-time freelancer, but celebrity portraits can also be taken in more informal settings. Visits to your area by politicians, sportsmen, TV stars, writers and artists will receive advance publicity in the local press. Some celebrities seem to spend most of their time opening supermarkets and charity events; being seen and photographed is very much part of their task.

There is a rapacious appetite in the media for celebrity photographs, though there are already a great number of photographers who spend their time on the publicity bandwagon, which makes it a highly competitive business.

There is also a specialised market in candid pictures of the famous, which is why the members of the Royal Family are followed everywhere by a small army of paparazzi photographers.

Most people do not object to being photographed; certainly the experience can be made more enjoyable if the photographer takes the trouble to print up a shot or two to give to his subjects. As one photographer has noted: 'It's good to *give* photographs as well as to *take* them.'

People are also curious to know why you want to take their photograph; it's a very reasonable request. And you ought to be able to give an adequate answer. If you can't then you should be thinking more clearly about your motives.

Some say these are unwarranted intrusions; others reckon that the famous are fair game for photographers anytime and anywhere. It does seem to be a rather grubby profession.

Children

A less antisocial activity is photographing children. It's probable that children occupy more frames of film than any other subject, yet very few of these 'memory maker' snaps will have any sales potential whatsoever. Too often children are told to stand still and look at the camera, which is guaranteed to produce static and unrevealing pictures. For the average child the sight of daddy getting out his camera merely produces a blank bored expression or a variety of funny faces. The more they are coaxed into compliance, the less likely that good photographs will result.

The demand for pictures of children is a good deal wider than 'mother and baby' magazines. People add an element of human interest to pictures of all kinds, and children provide an even more emotional response. But publishable pictures should show a good deal more than children grinning at the camera.

Children display such a wide range of emotions and expressions, going from one to another with bewildering speed. Unless you are tackling a formal portrait there is seldom any need to 'stage manage' photographic sessions, and the less attention you draw to yourself and your camera the more natural your pictures will be. Your subjects may be intrigued, initially, by your camera contortions; but most self-respecting kids will soon tire of your relentless knob-twiddling and lens-changing in order to get on with something more interesting.

The fly-on-the-wall approach means you can capture the unguarded, unposed moments that reveal so much about childhood. It's natural, of course, to begin with your own children, or children of immediate family and friends. No matter how familiar the scenario there is no reason why saleable pictures should not result, *provided* you are able to see the children through the eyes of a photographer rather than a parent.

Your pictures may have a very personal meaning for you, but picture buyers will generally be looking for photographs which represent aspects of childhood rather than portraits which characterise an individual child. For the family album, with memories in mind, we ask children to look at the camera and smile. While good portraits of this type may have some sales potential, better results are almost always obtained by allowing children to become absorbed in some activity so that the photographer can shoot virtually unobserved.

It's a good idea to try and divorce your own feelings for your subjects, so that you can illustrate the many aspects of childhood instead of merely shooting portraits. And remember that smiles are not mandatory: the greater variety of expressions you can capture, the more illustrative uses your pictures may prove to have.

Set-up Shots

There are a number of photographers who make a good living by setting up situation shots with groups of people, which are almost like stills from a film in which actors are taking on various roles. This kind of photography is demanding, requiring careful planning and location finding. And if it's hard enough to capture the right expression when photographing one person, it can be a nightmare getting a group of people to interact effectively. But it's this very difficulty that makes stock situation shots so saleable — usually to advertising and publicity markets.

These markets need a constant supply of pictures which purport to show typical people in typical situations: a family enjoying a picnic, a young couple having a meal in a restaurant, an elderly couple in their new retirement home. Such pictures may *appear* unposed, natural and typical; ironically, however, the natural look must be carefully orchestrated. The people must be attractive, the settings perfect and uncluttered. Most importantly the subjects' expressions must match the prevailing mood — almost always upbeat. It's for this reason that professional models (often 'character' models) are generally used for this kind of work. The expense of setting up shots may be considerable, but then so are the rewards for those photographers who succeed.

Insight: Stephen Hyde

Stephen Hyde collected a BA degree from London University five years ago. The subject was history, but by the time his student days were over it was photography that had captured his imagination. He worked as a photographer's assistant in London, while he built up a portfolio of portrait pictures. Since then he's been freelancing in London, and now works for a variety of clients — public relations, advertising, company reports and brochures — supplemented by more interesting (if less well-paid) jobs for Sunday supplements, women's magazines and other publications.

It's never easy to break into commercial photography, since many people are reluctant to give assignments to photographers without a proven track record. But what Stephen lacked in experience he made up for in initiative: in order to build up a portfolio of portraits he went to his local library, consulted *Who's Who*, and wrote to a number of the people he admired, asking if he could photograph them. Surprisingly, perhaps, at least half said yes . . .

'I said, in my letters, that I was a young photographer trying to get on. It could be that my approach appealed to people's vanity. It was certainly easier to photograph them after such a direct approach, since they had already made the psychological decision to sit for me. I was able to work without the pressures of a commercial assignment; if I made mistakes it didn't matter too much.

'Staying-power is very important for a freelance photographer. I started off with about a dozen pictures of famous people, which I showed to London art directors. You've got to have a go; it's no good holding back. You should be assertive even if that means taking on jobs that you feel may be beyond you, and giving them your best shot. Otherwise you'll never get anywhere.

'I can't stress too much the importance of putting a good portfolio together. It's better to invest money and time in doing that, rather

Portraiture is a demanding discipline—especially when the photographer is working on assignment and has only a short time to get his pictures. On location the subject's own home environment may throw up picture opportunities, but it's still advisable to arrive with a few pre-planned ideas. Stephen Hyde visited novelist J. P. Donleavy in Ireland, and a nearby stretch of water provided the setting for this moody portrait.

The eccentric composition, with the writer looking out over the water, is held together by the far horizon and the diagonal line of the water's edge. The viewer's eyes naturally gravitate towards the figure, then follow the writer's own gaze. (Photograph: Stephen Hyde) than buying fancy equipment — which you won't be able to use if you're not getting any work. Art directors see a lot of photographers every week, so you've got to make sure that its *your* name that sticks in their mind. Don't spread yourself too thinly by including too wide a range of pictures in your portfolio. Instead of including still life, fashion and portraiture, for example, it's probably better to concentrate on one branch of photography.

'It's important to develop your own style, while demonstrating that you are adaptable. If your style is too personal and idiosyncratic, then you may find yourself missing out on the more run-of-the-mill jobs. On the other hand, if you have no personal style at all then your pictures will not be very memorable. It can be hard to create a balanced portfolio which creates the required impression: that you are a good photographer who is eager to work. It's a good idea to fill your portfolio with pictures that show the subjects that you are most keen to tackle.

'As you progress with your photography you should keep your original objectives in mind. You may have achieved some successes, but you shouldn't be satisfied with that. Equally you should avoid becoming disillusioned. When I was starting out I was spurred on by something I read in a book; the gist of it was that when you get disheartened you should remember that there are a great number of magazines and books being published every day of the year. It's an all-consuming machine that eats up pictures. *Someone* has got to supply the pictures, and there's no reason why it shouldn't be *you.*

'There are thousands of photographers chasing the work, but equally the need for photography is almost insatiable. You need to build up your self-confidence by thinking positively. The classic beginner's mistake is to apologise for his photography. I can remember doing it myself, but there's really no point in being negative about your work when you are showing your portfolio, or pointing out how difficult the shots were to take.

'When an art director gives a job to a young photographer, you can be sure that *his* neck is on the line too. If you make a mess of your first assignment, then he will have some explaining to do to his superiors. So it's always a risk to give an assignment to an untried photographer. On the other hand, all art directors want to be the one who discovers the next photographic star . . .

Getting Ideas
'When I get a portrait assignment I give a great deal of thought to how to approach the job. I make sure I go in with one or two firm

ideas about particular shots: ideas which I can fall back on in case I'm short of inspiration on the day. So I'll think about composition, lighting, backdrops, etc. Sometimes I look through the work of other portrait photographers, such as Irving Penn. That may sound like plagiarism but I find it a useful way to help generate visual ideas.

'I may be a bit nervous about a shoot, and my subject may be wary about being photographed. It's all too easy to allow the photographic process to destroy the rapport and spontaneity that I like to foster. There's nothing worse than worrying about technicalities while you are trying to talk to your subject and establish a relationship. I'm always looking for a simple, relaxed photograph which reveals the character of the subject. That's the ideal. All I ask of the people I photograph is that they should be themselves and not put on a show for the camera

'I find it easier to work with black and white than with colour; lighting is always critical, of course, but it's especially so with colour transparency film. Black and white allows you to move quickly from one mood or location to another. You can respond immediately to new ideas. But with colour you generally have to decide on one main shot and set up your studio lights accordingly. This means you may have to ask your subject to come back after you've arranged everything. Black and white also allows you to add the finishing touches to a picture in the darkroom.

'Film format plays an important role in determining what kinds of pictures you will get. Some photographs are "taken" and some are "made": 35mm tends to produce the former while 5 × 4in necessitates a more formal approach; it makes for a photographic *event*. The medium-format Hasselblad camera suits my style of photography. I use daylight whenever possible, since my lighting techniques aren't as good as nature's yet. But when I shoot in colour I take along five Bowens Monolite flash units, umbrellas, soft boxes, etc. I might need them or I might not, but I always pack them in the car, just in case.'

Glamour

In popular folklore photographers are supposed to spend their time snapping scantily clad women; even carrying a camera can elicit a 'nudge nudge, wink wink' response. And in the words of an advertising pundit: 'A scantily clad girl will sell almost anything, and a scantily clad girl on a horse is even better.'

Sex sells. That's probably not the way it *should* be, but that's the way it *is*. The dictionary defines 'glamour' as 'delusive, alluring or exciting beauty or charm'. In photography the accent is generally on 'delusive': packaging a safe, sanitised aura of undemanding sexuality for a largely male audience.

The market for glamour photography is huge, since it can be combined, however incongruously, with any advertising campaign or marketing exercise that the fertile mind can imagine. Scantily dressed women are used to promote products as inappropriate as chain-saws and bulldozers. They smile enticingly out from page three, and lounge across the gatefolds of men's magazines. And you only have to glance through the titles on the top shelf of the newsagent to discover that hard-core pornography is alive and well and fuelling some truly gruesome and gynaecological fantasies.

The author will suspend his own reservations about glamour photography just long enough to give a few pointers. If you are going to shoot glamour then you might as well produce *good* glamour; as an example of what to avoid, take a look at the 'readers' wives' section of one of the men's magazines. Wives and girlfriends adopting ludicrous poses on a leatherette sofa in some suburban living room do not make saleable glamour . . .

The combination of inexperienced photographer and inexperienced model is a recipe for disaster. Their nervousness and inexpertise will be mutually contagious. For many photographers their first taste of glamour photography will be studio evenings at their local camera club — with a hired model, a battery of lights, a forest of tripods and a bunch of fellow photographers trying to bluff their way out of embarrassment. Such events will offer practice in setting up studio flash equipment, and running through a repertoire of poses, though they are unlikely to produce anything approaching saleable photographs.

There are studios in most towns where photographers can hire the facilities by the hour. Included in the price are likely to be studio lights, a choice of backdrops and props. Most studios will be able to supply professional or semi-professional models. For the 35mm

Glamour and nude photography covers a wide variety of approaches and styles, from the bland chumminess of 'Page 3' to the gratuitous exploitation of the porno magazines. It's a fine line between art and titillation, and most photographers settle unrepentantly for the latter, since there is a ready sale for this kind of material.

Photographs such as this one attempt to get away from the clichéd interpretations of the nude, though the nude in the landscape is threatening to become a cliché in its own right. The combination of womanly contours and the topography of the natural landscape can produce powerful compositions, even though sales potential is not great. For the full glamour treatment look no further than the top shelf in your local newsagent . . . (Photograph: R. Alison)

photographer it will often be possible to use the studio's own medium-format equipment for a further fee. Costs can naturally be kept down by sharing hire charges with other photographers.

A makeshift studio can be built in most homes, though lack of space may preclude full-length glamour pictures. Backdrops, props and lights soon make even the largest of rooms seem cramped. Remember too, that your model will probably have to stand a few feet in front of a backdrop to avoid casting ugly shadows.

Models

Finding models can be a problem. Hiring professionals will be a major expense unless good picture sales are immediately forthcoming. Amateur models will not be able to run nonchalantly through the whole gamut of glamour poses, but you will at least be able to hone your photographic techniques. Many young girls aspire to be models, and are as keen as photographers to build up a portfolio of pictures. If you can promise to supply a set of good prints — rather than cash — you may be able to develop a working relationship that's mutually beneficial.

Glamour photography needs careful planning, especially if good money is being laid out for a studio session. Professional models will be able to bring a selection of clothes; other ideas, props and backgrounds are the province of the photographer.

Before you even load your camera with film, you should have firmly in mind the appropriate markets for your pictures. A host of (largely unwritten) rules cover the field of glamour photography: poses and expressions that feature in the pages of men's magazines might not be appropriate for calendars or advertising shots. And magazine covers have, generally, to be less explicit than material contained within. Publications which have good overseas sales must monitor the use of glamour photographs, since many countries will ban — or mutilate — offending copies.

The seamlessly perfect fantasies of the men's magazines are published as sets: a series of, say, ten to twenty pictures showing a model fully clothed at first, with subsequent shots becoming more and more revealing. Locations can be either studio-based or outdoors, though much more is required of the photographer than simply to set up a sheet of background paper. Fantasies are fuelled by all the elements in the pictures, whether they be satin sheets in a makeshift 'boudoir' or the luxurious surroundings of a private swimming pool. If you know someone with a flash penthouse suite or other kind of home with photographic potential, then you need look no further for a glamour location. If not, then you'll need to improvise: a careful choice of backgrounds, clothes and props can compensate for other shortcomings in your choice of location. Outdoor glamour sets pose other problems, at least in Britain, with goose-pimples likely on any but the warmest of summer days. And there's no effects filter on the market that can magically transform a wind-swept British beach into some tropical paradise. Most outdoor glamour sets in the men's magazines have been shot abroad. Indoor shots can rely on imagination and artifice, but outdoors there is no faking the quality of light that is commonplace in sunnier climes.

Glamour sets should be erotic, without ever descending into pornography. The imagination itself is a powerful stimulant and a partially clothed model can often be more erotic than the same model nude. It's important to study the appropriate magazines to see just what kind of material they use. Some want sophistication and luxury, while others prefer to see 'girl-next-door' types in more down-to-earth surroundings.

Wide demand

The market for glamour is, however, a great deal wider than picture sets for the men's magazines. Single pictures are always in demand for editorial and advertising uses. Professional models will naturally know what to expect; they will probably have a wide selection of appropriate outfits, and will be very aware of how to emphasise their best features and disguise any physical shortcomings. They will also be able to run through a repertoire of standard 'glamour' poses with minimal prompting from the photographer.

These poses may seem a little hackneyed, and it is hard to avoid the clichéd approach. But much of the glamour market is quite old-fashioned: what's required is generally what was selling twenty years ago, with a nod towards current tastes in fashion. Models cavort on sunny beaches, pretend to throw beach balls towards the photographer, and peer enticingly through picturesque window frames. For this kind of pin-up photography the accent should be on the suggestive rather than the blatant. The difference may simply lie in the model's expression: the way she relates to the photographer and therefore to the viewer. The pin-up traditionally looks fit and cheerful, rather than sexually alluring.

Much has been written about the difference between nakedness and nudity and, while glamour pictures continue to sell and sell, there is a small but growing market for pictures which deal with the nude in ways that are arguably less exploitative. Posters, cards and calendars, for example, use good nude photography for its own sake, rather than to sell a product. This is one area where creative interpretations of the human form are applicable, and black and white photography is currently in vogue. As if to redress a few hundred years of artistic imbalance, there is also a genuine reply to the question 'Why no pictures of nude *men*?', and a number of photographers are rising to this challenge.

Landscapes

Most photographers find themselves shooting landscapes at one time or another. Yet the results are so often disappointing. A scene that seemed so stunning on the day of our visit may be translated into, well, just another photo.

The trouble is that our appreciation of the landscape is more than merely visual. We feel the warmth of the sun, hear the birds singing, sniff a little fresh air, feel grass instead of concrete beneath our feet and perhaps share our feelings with companions. The snapshots we take during a country walk are unlikely to recapture the intensity of these feelings; they are likely to be but the palest of imitations.

In fact it requires a good eye to transform a three-dimensional panorama into a two-dimensional slide or print. The landscape is a complex pattern of colour, tone, shape and line. The eye will pick out the salient details, but the camera gives equal weight to every element. So it's important to be very selective; in landscape photography what we leave out of a picture is as important as what we leave in.

Good landscapes will sell, though there is always stiff competition from specialist landscape photographers working with large-format equipment. And this is one area of photography where larger film formats traditionally have the edge over 35mm. Postcard, calendar and poster publishers will seldom look twice at transparencies smaller than 5 × 4in. Landscapes for magazine covers should be on roll-film or 5 × 4in, leaving 35mm shots for the inside pages.

This reluctance to use 35mm landscapes *is* beginning to break down, with the excellence of modern lenses and 35mm films, but if a picture editor is able to compare a 5 × 4in and a 35mm transparency on a light-box there is little doubt that he will plump for the greater resolving power and fine detail of the larger format.

Successful landscape photography is all about being in the right place at the right time. Apart from the weather, most of the factors are under our control: location, choice of viewpoint, season, time of day, format, film and lens combination, etc. Perhaps most important is our willingness to put ourselves out: to get out of our cars, go beyond the hackneyed view that everybody else shoots and be patient enough to wait for the light and weather conditions to change to our advantage.

Time of Day

Choosing the right time of day is particularly important. Too many photographers shoot their landscapes in the middle of the day, when the sun is high in the sky and the light at its most bland and unrevealing. Almost without exception more interesting pictures can be obtained early in the morning or late afternoon, and many of the landscape photographers whose work is most admired only work at these times.

A low sun emphasises texture and colour in the landscape, whereas midday light tends to reduce colour saturation. The difference between a passable shot and a highly saleable photograph may be nothing more than a couple of hours. You'll get better pictures than most other photographers if you simply get up *earlier* than they do.

Some of the best landscape photographs look as if they're the result of a lucky break, in capturing a special play of light. But if there is any luck in landscape photography then it always comes to those photographers who work the hardest. One stunning shot may be the reward for visiting a location time after time, waiting for all the elements to come together in the final definitive picture.

Wide-angle lenses are the immediate choice for landscape work. They emphasise space and distance, giving good separation between foreground and background. A few steps to one side by the photographer will change the composition dramatically. Including foreground details is one of photography's conventions; many shots need some device to hold the composition together and lead the viewer's eye into the rest of the picture.

Standard and telephoto lenses also have their place in landscape photography. Long lenses compress receding planes, so that a range of mountain peaks, for example, will be rendered as though they are stacked up one behind the other, almost like cardboard cut-outs. Telephoto lenses are excellent for picking out detail and simplifying a scene into a graphic composition of shape, tone and colour.

For many editorial uses landscapes have to be shot 'straight', but the atmospheric quality of this shot has been exaggerated by a bit of darkroom trickery. A red filter was used at the taking stage. During printing, a diffusing filter was mounted beneath the enlarger lens. This makes darker areas of the picture 'bleed' into the lighter areas, while leaving the tones of the stormy sky more or less unchanged. The sombre mood was emphasised further by printing heavily onto a hard, contrasty grade of printing paper.

A Strong Support

There's one accessory which will improve the quality of landscape photography like no other. A tripod is an awkward beast to carry, especially in the landscape, but it's remarkable what a difference it can make to the resulting pictures. Firstly, with the camera secured on a tripod the full range of films can be used, including the slowest and most grain-free. Choice of usable apertures is equally wide, since shutter speeds can run a great deal longer than the 1/30sec that is the limit of most people's ability to hold a camera steady: f/16 at 8 seconds? No problem at all if you have a tripod . . .

There is now a bewildering variety of special effects filters on sale, and it's a simple matter to use one to give a soft, diffused atmosphere to a landscape. But filters can become habit-forming; if you are forever using graduated filters to punch a bit of false colour into an uninspiring sky, then you are over-reliant on artifice. In any case, filters cannot recreate the subtlety of natural light and colour. Instead of reaching for a gadget it is generally better to be patient and wait for the light to change.

In this tranquil scene a filter might have produced the misty background, but it would have affected the foreground too. Instead the natural conditions have been used to separate the foreground details of fence, tree and sheep from the rest of the picture. (Photograph: Malc Birkitt)

Secondly, a tripod allows a composition to be fine-tuned until it includes exactly as much as the photographer wants, and no more. It's a matter of moments to ensure that distant horizons are rendered perfectly horizontal.

Lightweight tripods are almost a contradiction in terms, like a bicycle with square wheels. To support even a 35mm camera in a stiff breeze a tripod should be as sturdy as possible, with rigid legs that can be braced for extra strength. Some of the cheaper and flimsier models actually *introduce* camera shake rather than eliminate it!

Thirdly, a tripod will get the very best out of your lenses in terms of crisp focus and overall sharpness. Get the sturdiest tripod you can afford; as a once-in-a-lifetime investment it will improve your landscape photography beyond recognition. Don't be put off by the extra weight you'll be carrying; if the gadget pack is overloaded then leave a few lenses at home instead. And if you and your tripod are out in the landscape at first light, you'll also be able to dispense with a lot of effects filters, since dawn light brings more subtle interplays of colour than can ever be achieved with a square of plastic.

There are trends and fashions in landscape photography, as there are in every other branch of the medium. It's important to research the markets to which you hope to sell pictures. The greetings card companies still rely greatly on traditional scenes which elicit an immediate and emotive response: snowy mountains, seascapes, sunsets, etc. The postcard market also uses a great deal of such pictures, though current trends are towards more creative landscape interpretations. A few years ago black and white postcards and posters were unsaleable; now monochrome photography is enjoying a deserved revival. The general public are, after all, accustomed to seeing more sophisticated imagery these days.

Insight: Simon Warner

Simon Warner is a freelance photographer specialising in the landscape — particularly of the north of England. He has had no formal photographic training, but a postgraduate course in film and TV techniques prompted a desire to take up stills photography; and a spell in London made him realise just how much he loved the countryside. Magazine assignments took him all over Britain, and these travels began his now extensive collection of landscape photographs.

Simon now lives in Yorkshire and runs his photographic business from a converted farmhouse. His work includes the marketing of landscape photographs through his own picture library and shooting commissions for a wide range of clients, including publishers, advertising agencies, magazines and the travel trade. He has plenty of good advice about the shooting and selling of landscape photographs, culled from more than ten years of freelancing.

'I really started out as an enthusiastic amateur, with my interest being in black and white photography. So for many years my growing collection of landscape pictures was shot only in black and white, without too much thought for the future. If I had the chance to do it all over again I would shoot everything in colour, and double up in black and white for some of the pictures. It should be easy to change from colour to black and white, but there are crucial differences between the two which go deeper than the obvious ones of exposure. There's a bigger problem of creative attitude.

'There are also many kinds of landscape photography. On one level it's merely a matter of topographical recording; on another level you have what has become known as chocolate-box pictures, which aren't highly regarded outside that particular market — even though they are difficult to shoot. I try to take landscapes which are

London-based photographers have an unfair advantage over their provincial counterparts in many aspects of commercial photography. London is, after all, where the majority of picture buyers are. But the landscape photographer may find that access to his chosen subject matter is more important than a London address, especially if he hopes to sell a good deal of his work via picture libraries.

Proximity to the landscape allows the photographer to return again and again to a particular area — in different seasons and lighting conditions — which is a luxury denied to the photographer with only a limited time to cover a landscape assignment. There is an element of luck involved in getting good light for landscape photography but, as in other areas of photography, the harder you work the luckier you seem to get! (Photograph: Simon Warner)

more interesting than chocolate-box pictures, but which will still fit into the other commercial markets.

'For years I used 35mm film exclusively, though I should have realised earlier that there were advantages to using larger formats. I seldom use 5 × 4in film, unlike a lot of landscape photographers. I tend to work with roll-film and a Mamiya 6 × 7cm camera. The rectangular format gives greater flexibility for landscapes than the standard square format. The camera has a revolving back, so you never need to hold the camera on its side, and the 6 × 7cm format means you can print on 10 × 8in paper without having to crop the image.

'The variability of the British climate makes landscape photography exciting; you can never really predict what the weather is going to do next. But I do listen to the weather forecasts, and often phone the weather centre to get more information about the weather in locations I plan to visit. If I'm visiting a place for the first time I'll take a look at all the postcards I find on sale. They can give me some good ideas about what are regarded as the best viewpoints.

Commissions

'I take a lot of pictures for myself, in the hope that they will have commercial potential later — perhaps through library sales. Otherwise I work on commissions to shoot particular landscapes for individual clients. It's a good way of working, though such jobs aren't two-a-penny. The discipline of working for someone else is quite attractive after working on your own.

'I find myself doing a lot of tourism photography, which generally involves photographing people in the countryside. At first I didn't set these pictures up, but that used to be difficult: people seldom come into shot in the exact way you want. I realised that it can actually be easier to go to the trouble of setting these pictures up quite elaborately, with models. You come away with better pictures.

'My collection of landscape pictures has grown over the years, so I can market the work myself. I don't spend a great deal of money publicising my library pictures, but I'm in the Yellow Pages and appear in one or two of the creative and media publications that run free listings of photographers. However, I seem to get very few new contacts from these listings. More productive is a paid advertisement in one of the photographic directories; that seems to elicit quite a bit of response from outside the region.

'When you work on your own — and outside London — it's difficult to find the time to take the pictures, process them, do all the office work and continue to market your pictures. You just gradually widen your contacts in the markets for landscape photography and try to keep up to date with new developments. I get a lot of calls from picture researchers, so I am able to hear about the new books that are being planned. And I like to be sent picture request lists, when books are being put together. You have to work quite hard to keep your name in people's minds, especially when the people in publishing change jobs so regularly. Books interest me more than anything else, and I've already produced two books with my wife, who is a writer. I also contribute a lot of pictures to other people's books.

'Landscape photography is one of the branches of the medium that can be tackled successfully by people who live outside London. There is great competition in this field, however; I have to compete with a number of excellent landscape photographers for every commission.'

Nature

The market for natural history photographs is vast. From the winsome, frolicking kittens which adorn chocolate-box lids to the specialist demands of micro-photography, nature pictures are always in demand. Magazines and books featuring the natural world proliferate. There are even specialist picture libraries which deal only in nature subjects: birds, botany and insects, for example.

While the demand for suitable pictures is voracious, the supply is equally large, and a number of talented photographers make a good living within one specialised branch of natural history work. The work can be demanding, requiring a solid grasp of photographic technique and a good knowledge of the subject, as well as the patience that is often needed when photographing wild creatures.

A good starting point is domestic, farm and zoo animals. The photographer can refine his vision and technique with animals that will be co-operative at best, and at worst conveniently confined. It takes a good deal of practice, for example, to freeze animals in motion; better to perfect the techniques with the family pet than make costly mistakes on location with wild animals.

Zoos offer excellent opportunities for photographing many species at close quarters, and many publishable pictures may be taken. The drawback is that, naturally enough, the cages and pens are built to keep animals in rather than to allow access to photographers. Bars and wire netting can play havoc with camera-work, and photographers will be forced to stand some distance away.

In many circumstances a telephoto or zoom lens will be needed to bridge these distances, giving only a small depth of focus. This can be to the photographer's advantage, since netting close to the camera will be blurred in the resulting pictures if a large lens

Nature photography demands both immaculate photographic technique and a great deal of patience. Few wild creatures are obliging enough to pose for the camera; most regard man with understandable suspicion. Standards in nature photography have risen enormously in recent years, thanks to technological advances in branches of the medium such as micro-photography and high-speed flash. Prices have risen too, with much specialised equipment beyond the pocket of the average freelance.

But the imaginative photographer thinks more about what he *can* do, rather than fretting about what he *can't*. Shots like this can be taken with a macro lens and one — or perhaps two — flashguns. Such pictures should be well captioned: species (and Latin name), location and any other relevant details. (Photograph: Derek Sayer) aperture is used. It's possible to poke long lenses through some wire barriers for a totally uninterrupted view if this is allowed.

Forward-looking zoos try to give their animals a habitat that is as natural as possible. Prison bars are giving way to more open enclosures which allow animals to roam freely and photographers to get better pictures. By carefully selecting suitable viewpoints and backgrounds it is possible to produce pictures that look as though they were taken in the wild.

Safari parks take the idea of open enclosures one step further. If anything it is the paying public which is caged, while the animals move around freely. Drivers are instructed to keep their car windows closed. Take heed of the warning; an inquisitive monkey might treat your expensive camera, lens and motor-drive with less than due respect! A clean car window, with the camera lens pressed up close to the glass, will allow photographs to be taken freely.

Captive animals can provide interesting — and often humorous — pictures, but there are many reasons why a photographer should heed the call of the wild. Zoos and safari parks attempt to give their animals as much freedom as possible, but the bottom line is that they are not free to live their lives as they would in the wild. Zoo animals become institutionalised. They have no predators and no need to hunt for food; their rations arrive every day courtesy of the zoo-keepers. Their behaviour, in short, is very different from what it would be in the wild. And, with animal photography, it is often the behavioural aspects that make a picture saleable: feeding, courtship, mating, nesting, displaying, etc.

The flora and fauna of this country is rich and various, though many of us go through life ignoring it. Most wildlife photographers have an abiding interest in the natural world, and see picture-taking opportunities that the non-naturalist would probably not notice.

Creatures of Habit

Birds, for example, are notoriously difficult to photograph, and successful shots come from careful planning. Most species are wary of man, and won't sit still while a photographer fiddles with his f/stops. But they are also creatures of habit and investigations of these habits will allow the photographer to tip the odds in his direction. Many birds have favourite vantage points for singing or displaying; others can be attracted to a particular place with the appropriate food. Nesting sites will see much to-ing and fro-ing as birds first incubate the eggs and then feed their young.

When birds are preoccupied with these rituals the photographer can operate from convenient cover, or a camouflaged hide.

Bird photographs may almost be portraits of individual birds, or they may illustrate some characteristic behavioural trait. All will have sales potential if they are sharp, well composed and uncluttered. Pictures of rare species will have specialist applications, but that does not rule out the common garden birds.

Much the same applies to other animals: a little knowledge of animal behaviour will pay dividends. In most situations the photographer needs to be hidden; at the very least he needs to be still and wearing clothes that blend in with his surroundings.

Another option is to trigger a camera by remote control: a simple task with today's electronic triggering devices. A remote camera can be used when an event can be predicted: such as a kingfisher which habitually fishes from one riverside branch, or a fox attracted to food which the photographer regularly puts out. An unmanned camera has to be pre-focused on a particular spot and the exposure set; once the animal comes within range the photographer can fire the shutter from a distance. The use of a motor-drive allows more pictures to be taken immediately, though the whirring noise may tend to drive a lot of animals away.

Triggering devices can be as simple as an air release: depressing a small rubber bulb makes compressed air fire the shutter at a distance of many yards. Infra-red triggers can perform a similar task over bigger distances, and no direct contact is required between photographer and camera.

Any photographer worthy of the name should treat the wild creatures in his viewfinder with respect. Many species are already under threat, and the actions of thoughtless photographers can only hasten their demise. Photographers should work as unobtrusively as possible, particularly when shooting at breeding sites. If, for example, a photographer cuts down foliage to give an uninterrupted view of a bird's nest, he may give an equally uninterrupted view to one of the bird's predators. Do not, in short, endanger the well-being of any animal, rare or common, for the sake of a photograph.

Knowledge of the subject is seldom as important as in nature photography. Pictures must be backed up with comprehensive captions if they are to sell, especially if they are offered through a picture library. Subjects must be accurately identified (English *and* Latin names, if possible) and there are many other details which may be relevant. The location may be important, especially if the photograph shows an endangered species. And if it illustrates some aspect of animal behaviour, then full details should be given. The more comprehensive the caption, the more saleable the picture.

Travel

Not too many years ago it was only the well heeled who could afford to take regular holidays abroad. Now it seems that two weeks in the sun are a yearly ritual for the majority of the population. And not always on the Costa Blanca: places like Sri Lanka, Bali and the Seychelles are not just exotic faraway names on the map; they are now regular ports of call for today's more adventurous tourists.

There are many photographers working full-time in the field of travel and location photography. They may work directly for the travel companies, who need a constant flood of pictures for their brochures. Freelance photographers may market the pictures themselves, or collaborate with a picture agency.

Travel photography sounds like heaven—roaming the world with a bag full of cameras. And it certainly offers more excitement than shooting pots and pans for mail-order catalogues. But, as any travel photographer will stress, it is also very hard work. Rising at dawn and shooting till sundown makes for a busy working day.

The part-time freelance photographer is unlikely to be able to afford the time or the money to take regular photographic jaunts to all points of the globe. But family holidays will offer plenty of opportunities to chronicle another country and culture in pictures with sales potential. At the very least they will provide evidence of skills for a portfolio of travel photographs.

It matters little where you go; more important is the thought and imagination you bring to the task. The markets for travel and location photography require pictures of every type—not just 'mug-shots' of major landmarks such as the Eiffel Tower or the Colosseum. Picture libraries are overflowing with the obvious visual clichés, while many other saleable images are there for the taking.

Travel photography can incorporate a wide variety of subject

Travel photography involves more than just shooting the well-known landmarks and beauty spots. There are creative opportunities around every corner for recording interesting aspects of everyday life, which can reveal more about different countries and cultures than statues and monuments ever can. It's always a good idea to do a little research before travelling; guidebooks and maps can produce many picture ideas, and save valuable time when actually on location. But there will always be many pictures that cannot be pre-planned: happy accidents that come to the photographer who keeps his eyes open and camera at the ready.

It's the photographer's responsibility to ensure that he does not intrude unnecessarily into people's lives. He should respect cultural and religious values which may differ from his own, and learn when it's acceptable to take pictures. This shot shows a street scene on the Greek island of Rhodes. (Photographer: John Russell)

matter: reportage, portraiture, architecture, landscape, glamour — even still life. A few examples may help to stimulate further ideas.

People pictures are a must, whatever the location. Locals can be pictured at work and at leisure, enjoying a carnival, producing local crafts; visitors sunning themselves on sandy beaches, enjoying a meal out, visiting beauty spots. The tone, for the tourist trade at least, has to be unrelentingly upbeat. It's an unwritten rule that holiday-makers should look cheerful, and that skies should be blue and the sun shining.

Sod's Law will no doubt dictate that your working holiday will be blighted by leaden skies; such are the frustrations of travel photography . . .

Architecture will naturally take in well-known landmarks, though it's to the photographer's advantage to look for the unusual viewpoint, the telling composition. This is usually a matter of wearing out shoe-leather rather than fancy lenses or effects filters. However, the character of a town or a country may be captured as effectively by seeking out less celebrated — but more typical — subjects.

Forward Planning

Even with today's cheap flights and package holidays, it's still important to use your time and energies most effectively. A little planning and research undertaken *before* a trip will ensure that you have plenty of picture ideas to shoot as soon as you reach your destination. It's frustrating to arrive home again, only to realise that you have missed a lot of pictures through sheer ignorance of the place you visited.

Much relevant information can be gleaned from holiday brochures, tourist guides and books. Make notes of events and locations within easy reach, so you will have a provisional schedule to use once you arrive at your destination.

There's planning needed, too, in the matter of equipment. While it's increasingly easy to travel around the world, there are many countries in which you may have difficulties getting hold of fresh film, or getting them processed to a professional standard. And if you drop your only camera into a rockpool, you may spend the rest of the trip trying to get it repaired.

Equipment for a trip should be chosen with care, since there's always a temptation to take more gear than you will need. A basic outfit might include one 35mm camera body, plus wide-angle, standard and short telephoto lens, though a wide-to-tele zoom lens is a convenient alternative to carrying interchangeable lenses. An extra camera body is a worthwhile insurance policy against the chance that your photography will grind to a halt through camera malfunction.

It's also convenient for each camera body to be loaded with a different film: colour transparency and black and white, perhaps, or fast and slow emulsions to take care of whatever lighting conditions may be encountered.

A flashgun, mini-tripod and filters may complete the hardware.

116

Leave plenty of room for film, since it's wise to take all the rolls you expect to need. Your preferred stock may be either unobtainable — or horrendously expensive — where you are planning to go.

This will be enough to carry, on what may be primarily a family holiday. If, however, you are able to devote much of your trip to photography, then a greater proportion of your weight allowance could be given over to photographic equipment. For many markets roll-film formats are preferred to 35mm, so a 6 × 6cm or 645 outfit would almost certainly produce pictures that are more readily saleable.

A tripod, cumbersome as it is, will allow you to work morning till night, and come back with shots that just aren't possible with a hand-held camera. A camera case, whether soft or hard, will keep your gear safe and separate from your other luggage. If it's of manageable proportions you'll be able to keep it with you during plane flights, instead of consigning it to the baggage hold.

Film Protection

Airports are the bane of all travellers, but they present special hazards to the photographer on the move, in the shape of X-ray machines. In the fight against hijackers they are used to scan the contents of cases automatically; unfortunately the X-rays may have a detrimental effect on both exposed and unexposed film cassettes, with faster films being especially at risk. Keep films in your hand baggage and ask for them to be searched by hand. Some of the officials you see will comply with your request but others won't, in which case you'll have to cross your fingers as precious films are subjected to the dreaded rays.

Lead-lined pouches can be bought which are supposed to protect films from damage by X-rays, though many airport security staff would be tempted to increase the X-ray dosage when confronted by such an impenetrable container.

Travel is generally thought to be a good way to broaden the mind, though when you see the British laying waste to the Mediterranean holiday resorts you begin to wonder . . . Photographers have a special responsibility to respect the laws and customs of the countries they visit. Candid photography is an intrusive activity wherever you go; in some places, such as Islamic countries, this sense of intrusion will be felt more keenly. Photographers should be sensitive enough to realise when it's acceptable to shoot pictures and when it's better to put the camera away. Many Third-World countries are thronged with photographers; don't be surprised to find that many of the people you photograph will demand a small payment for the privilege.

It can be surprisingly easy to fall foul of local officialdom. You may have a perfectly rational reason for taking photographs, though your explanations may fall on deaf ears. For example, only a fool would venture near military installations with a camera in Iron Curtain countries! Photography is not always viewed as a totally innocent occupation. Think of yourself as a guest in the country you're visiting, and you won't go far wrong.

Sport

Religion might once have been 'the opium of the masses', but today it's probably sport that fits the bill. Not too many years ago the newspapers covered soccer, cricket, rugby, golf, tennis and very little else. Now there are dozens of sports which attract the media spotlight.

Snooker players, for example, used to compete for the world championship in some dingy hall, with only a trophy and pocket money at stake. These days the immaculately coiffured contestants stage their marathon finals for the television cameras, with enormous cash prizes riding on the result. When did you last hear the adage that proficiency at snooker is the sign of a mis-spent youth?

Television has been the principal agent in bringing so-called minority sports into the big-time. Badminton, squash, hockey, basketball, table tennis and darts are among the sports which attract a new armchair audience. As if that weren't enough we are happy to import even more from abroad, so that the razzmatazz of American football is a regular ingredient in our weekend viewing.

Gates at soccer matches may be declining steadily, but sport is avidly followed nonetheless — both on television and reported in the daily press, where still pictures help to bring some sense of an event's excitement and immediacy to our daily reading. Specialist magazines proliferate too, covering the entire sporting spectrum.

These publications closely reflect current trends, and many disappear from the bookstands as soon as interest begins to wane. Where are the skateboard magazines of yesteryear? Within this ever-changing scene there are many gaps that freelance photo-graphers can fill, but it's important to understand where those gaps are.

The newspapers treat sport like any other news, in that staff

119

Some photographers find that achieving crisp focus is difficult at the best of times, and a speedway meeting—with a crush of riders raising the dust—is certainly *not* the best of times! But race action is never random. In speedway, for example, the riders steer a very tight line around the course, so that photographers can easily pick the most advantageous viewpoint.

One competitor can be followed with the camera. This panning technique can produce crisp focus of the subject with a blurring to the background: the exact result will depend on the shutter speed used and the photographer's ability to match the speed of the rider with his camera. Alternatively, the photographer may prefer to pre-focus on a section of the course which is likely to produce plenty of action. In this shot the sense of speed is conveyed by the leading rider rounding the bend, with the other two bikers hard on his heels. (Photograph: Martyn Barnwell)

photographers are dispatched to cover important matches and meetings. The difference is simply that, unlike most other news stories, sports events don't just happen out of the blue. The timings of test matches, cup finals and other major competitions are known months, or even years, ahead.

The strength of much sports coverage is topicality. Readers can actually see a winning goal being scored, or an athletic slip catch held, remarkably soon after the event. Deadlines for sports pictures are often so tight that a photographer sitting behind the goal-line at a football match may only have the first fifteen minutes to grab his pictures, before the film cassettes are rushed to the paper's darkroom by dispatch rider.

Accredited sports photographers are issued with passes, enabling them to shoot from advantageous positions near to the action. In many sports this effectively rules out picture-taking by photographers without recognised passes. Few publishable football pictures are shot from the middle of the grandstand!

Part-time photographers have to face up to the fact that they will be unable to compete with accredited photographers at many events. Fortunately there is more to sports photography than this immediate news-gathering aspect. Instead of worrying about where they *can't* go, freelances should take advantage of situations and events where they *are* welcomed. And there are more timeless pictures to take: pictures that say something about the sport itself, instead of just recording a newsworthy moment that will have next to no sales potential a week after the event.

Practice

In capturing sporting action, practice really does make perfect. Before you can hope to make regular picture sales it's vital to cover as many different sporting events as possible. The technical side of sports photography has to be learned so thoroughly that it becomes second-nature to pan the camera and follow an athlete, or to pre-focus on a particular spot in anticipation of an action such as a horse jumping a fence.

In every sport there are peaks of the action: moments when the participants are at full stretch; moments that, when caught on film, provide a dynamic visual interpretation of the scene. A line of runners stretched out along the cinder track may not fire the imagination like those same runners bursting from the blocks as the starter fires his gun.

A pole-vaulter may be pictured just after the pole is slammed into the box: the pole is bent like a banana as the vaulter begins his ascent. Or the photographer may choose to shoot a second later, when the vaulter is scraping over the bar and, briefly, is almost stationary. Successful photographs of a sport such as motorcycle scrambling rely more on the photographer walking the course before the event to find camera positions which are likely to yield the most exciting pictures. A tight bend, a slippery gully or an unavoidable water hazard might fit the bill. The closer he can get to the riders the more immediate his pictures are likely to be, and the less he will have to rely on telephoto lenses and the difficulties associated with focusing them on fast-moving action.

It helps greatly to be familiar with the sport to be photographed, so that the photographer can put himself in the participants' shoes and work out the best vantage points. Sporting highlights cannot be orchestrated; the photographer has to make his own luck by deciding where and when the sporting elements are most likely to come together in a way that can be captured on film.

These matters will often be largely dictated by the organisers of an event. Many excellent camera positions may be out of bounds to spectators, for reasons of safety or to avoid participants being disturbed by clicking cameras and whirring motor-drives. For example, there are strict rules in operation during golf tournaments, dictating that pictures can only be taken when the golfers have completed their swings. A sudden noise while a golfer is lining up an important putt may be enough to disturb his concentration.

There are similar restrictions in many indoor events, such as snooker, and, equally often, a blanket ban on the use of flashguns. With so much money and prestige riding on the results of many sporting contests, it's a foolish photographer who disregards these restrictions.

Other problems have more photographic origins. A combination of low light and rapid action force a photographer to think carefully about the correct choice of film and hardware.

Appropriate Films

Fast film (ASA 400 or faster) will allow shorter shutter times, but fine detail will be sacrificed and grain will be more prominent. Slow films offer good definition and colour saturation, but may require the photographer to shoot at wide aperture: a practice which makes crisp focus ever more difficult to attain.

All sports photographers are faced with this basic dilemma, and it's a situation which really sorts out the men from the boys. One option — open only to staff photographers and freelancers with a healthy bank account — is to invest in an ultra-fast telephoto lens. A 300mm lens with a maximum aperture of f/2.8 is a popular lens, and a type made by many camera manufacturers and independent lens-makers. They can make the difference between getting an acceptable shot and not getting one at all, but they are big, bulky and horrendously expensive. An outlay of £1,500 (or more) is justifiable only for those freelancers who specialise in sports photography and who can boast regular picture sales.

A sport like boxing throws up a number of problems for photographers. A combination of harsh lighting, deep shadows, rapid movement inside the ring and restricted shooting positions for the photographer outside — all these criteria make it vital to choose the right equipment and film. A lens with large maximum aperture will allow the photographer to make the best of the lighting conditions, if the use of flash is frowned upon. It is easier to use a standard or wide-angle lens from the ringside than to shoot from afar with a telephoto or zoom.

Add a fast film (perhaps uprated to a higher ASA number, and later given extended development) to get a better chance of getting sharp pictures. An auto-wind or motor-drive can be useful, but offers no guarantees of capturing the decisive moment. (Photograph: Mick Rouse)

A general rule — especially for colour transparencies — is to shoot on the slowest film possible. Many experienced sport photographers shoot almost exclusively on Kodachrome 64. They are able to produce stunning results on such an unforgivingly slow emulsion by critical focus, picking the peaks of the action and, it must be said, by shooting a lot of film! If low light rules out such a slow film, then there are other transparency films which offer greater speed and which can, if necessary, be 'pushed' further to get acceptable results in poor light.

An autowind or motor-drive is a useful accessory in the sports photographer's gadget bag, though a 'mechanical thumb' cannot be relied upon to get the most telling picture. Even with continuous shooting it's possible to get a dozen shots which don't quite make the grade; a single shot, timed by the photographer, may be more successful.

The aspiring sports photographer should build up a portfolio of pictures from local events, honing his skills so that he can confidently tackle a variety of assignments. Gaining access to advantageous camera positions may require an approach to the event organisers, well in advance of the day.

With a small photographic staff many local papers will be interested in having sporting events covered by a freelance. Get in touch with the editor and offer to attend weekend events that might otherwise be passed over. The payment for your services is unlikely to be overly generous, but many well-known sports photographers started their careers in this way.

Specialist sports magazines are another market worth trying. While local newspapers need pictures to accompany up-to-the-minute news items, monthly periodicals take a different tack. Since they cannot compete with the daily press on topicality, they will devote space to longer features: profiles of sportsmen and women, in-depth coverage of major events, etc. For the photographic content many sports magazines rely to a great extent on freelancers who can either cover a particular sport or area of the country.

Pictures will not merely focus on the famous faces, however, and there is good sales potential for less specific pictures that simply show enthusiastic people enjoying sporting activities: a group of anglers huddled beneath their green umbrellas, the massed start of a charity 'fun run', a cricket match on the village green or a windsurfer catching a sea breeze.

All sporting pictures need careful captioning, and relevant notes should be taken at the time of shooting. Professional sportsmen need to be accurately identified, as should the venue, title of event, date and any other information which might make the picture more saleable to a chosen market.

GETTING ORGANISED

Choosing Cameras

Equipment is a notoriously difficult issue for the hobbyist photographer: an obsession with amassing more and more pieces of matt-black hardware is something that most photographers will admit to feeling at one time or another. The constant launches of much-vaunted new cameras can bring on attacks of neurosis in otherwise level-headed people. No matter what equipment they buy, there is bound to be something else on the market next month which will offer a more substantial helping of whizz-bang technology.

The rationale behind this chapter is to sort out the necessary items from the gadgets and frippery that serve no other real purpose than to part the gullible punter from his hard-earned cash. It is hoped, too, that the reader will be reassured about the probable suitability of the equipment he already owns for most assignments he is likely to undertake. It's pointless, after all, to spend money on inessentials which could more fruitfully be spent on film.

Many of the photographs we admire have been shot on equipment that the average hobbyist would regard as being rudimentary and old-fashioned. They might also have been printed with a geriatric enlarger in a makeshift darkroom under the stairs. Interviews with successful photographers constantly show this to be true. The end-product — transparency or print — is what matters; few people, outside the readers of photographic magazines, are interested in how they were made.

This is not to suggest that we should adopt a Luddite approach when considering new equipment, or turn our backs on genuine technological advances. The problem is merely to sort out the genuine from the sham, and choose our equipment with an objective eye to the job in hand rather than merely lusting after some all-singing, all-dancing machine with more flashing lights than Piccadilly Circus!

There are one or two important criteria to consider when deciding on a new camera or system. Don't expect too much help from manufacturers' brochures, since no one stays in business by pointing out the defects and drawbacks of their equipment.

Image Quality

The first priority — and perhaps the most difficult to evaluate — is image quality. Too many people base their choice of camera on the number of knobs and dials on the camera body, forgetting that the body is basically only a light-tight box to accommodate various lenses. It's surely a false economy to invest heavily in an expensive camera body, only to add sub-standard lenses and filters.

Trying out different cameras in a shop will tell you a great deal about their various handling characteristics, but nothing at all about their ability to resolve images crisply and accurately. You might be able to persuade the shop assistant to let you run a roll of film through a demonstration camera, but unless you mount it firmly on a tripod you won't know whether to put down any resulting 'softness' to camera-shake or poor lens quality.

So what do we do? Talking to experienced photographers will reveal their own favourite cameras and lenses: as good a guide as any, except that different photographers will recommend different makes. You will find, however, that a handful of manufacturers' names will crop up with monotonous regularity. Suffice it to say that cameras and optics from the 'big names' of the business are unlikely to disappoint. The fact is that standards are very high. Slight differences in lens performance matter little when compared, say, to the results achieved by using a tripod whenever possible.

The matter of reliability becomes vital once you start using your camera to make money. Breakdowns and malfunctions can be merely irritating or — if you are miles away from home — totally disastrous. Even the very best of cameras have been known to fail, and you can be sure it will be at the most awkward moment!

Many photographers swear by purely manual cameras; ie those that do not rely on batteries. But battery failure is no problem for those photographers with the foresight to carry a spare set of batteries in their gadget bag. More relevant, perhaps, is the robustness of cameras and lenses, allowing them to throw off everyday knocks without injury. Most of the big camera manufacturers offer at least one model built to the standards demanded by working professionals.

Metal, rather than plastics, predominate in these models.

In many branches of photography there are conventions which should be observed, if picture sales are to follow. In show-jumping, for example, there is usually just one, very brief, moment when horse and rider look their best as they negotiate a jump. If the shutter is pressed a fraction of a second too soon or too late, the results will be disappointing. This shot shows the rider in full control, and the horse about to clear the fence. The power and movement of the horse are vividly suggested, all four legs are off the ground, and the rider's face can be clearly seen.

A motor-drive is a useful accessory for the sports and action photographer, but it offers no guarantee that the 'decisive moment' will be captured. Even at a speed of, say, five frames per second, it is easy to miss the peak of the action. It's better to practise getting it right on a single frame—learning to anticipate when all the elements of a picture are likely to come together. After all, when you *see* the picture exactly as you want it, you are already too late to get the shot! (Photograph: Martyn Barnwell)

Leakproof gaskets keep sand, water and other unwanted 'foreign bodies' out of the vulnerable internal workings. They will be the most adaptable models in the range, able to take the fastest motor-drives and a bewildering array of accessories. They will also be significantly more expensive than most of a manufacturer's other cameras — an expense that may easily be justified by their 'built to last' construction.

Versatility is important. Your photography, at present, may require little in the way of specialised equipment. But this situation may change. You may, for example, become interested in action photography — for which a top shutter speed of 1/4,000sec would be very useful. Does the camera you are considering allow you to use the widest possible range of film? Could you uprate a film to ISO 3,200 and set this value on the camera body? Can you lock the mirror up, for vibration-free exposures?

You may want to try multiple exposures: recording two or more images on the same frame of film. Does your proposed camera have a multiple-exposure button, which cocks the shutter without moving the film forward? Do the available lenses include everything from fish-eye to super-telephoto optics? How about a perspective control lens for the budding architectural photographer? And so on . . .

You have to make a decision about how your photography might progress in future, and choose your equipment accordingly. Mistakes can be costly: if you decide your camera system is not sufficiently versatile then you will weep at the price you will be offered for your now second-hand gear. The moment you leave the camera shop with your new purchase it will be worth less than two-thirds of what you paid for it.

Film Formats

The great format debate has been heatedly discussed for as long as photography has been a talking point, and it shows no signs of being resolved. For many people the debate is decided on cost alone, since 35mm is the largest format they can realistically afford, while still paying off the mortgage and buying shoes for the kids. If this is your position, worry not: 35mm is now the accepted standard for a great deal of editorial photography. The quality of cameras, films and lenses has improved so dramatically over recent years that top-notch 35mm shots can be plastered over a magazine spread without any qualms about sharpness or definition.

Also 35mm cameras have wider wide-angles and longer telephotos in their lens ranges than any other format, since it's the burgeoning amateur market that has allowed rapid developments in optical design. Ever-increasing sales of 35mm SLRs have also brought prices down to the point where a modest outfit can be bought for less than the average weekly wage. Another advantage is that 35mm is highly portable: everything that might be needed for a day's shoot can be carried comfortably in a shoulder bag.

It's the diminutive size of a 35mm negative or transparency, however, which makes successful shooting an exacting business. Using slow films and a tripod, it's possible to produce images of exceptional sharpness, but the slightest softness will be translated, when greatly enlarged for reproduction, into an unacceptably blurred or woolly picture. Yet it's the convenience and versatility of 35mm that makes it such a useful tool; mounting your camera on a tripod destroys spontaneity and the ability to react rapidly to a changing situation.

Unless it is projected, a 35mm transparency is difficult to 'read', and most photographers do not scrutinise their photographs as closely as the average picture editor will. But it's a skill that must be acquired if repeated picture sales are to follow. Discrepancies come simply to light when printing from black and white negatives, but transparencies need to be scanned with a magnifying loupe. Spots, processing marks, scratches, errors in focus and exposure: find any of these and you have a cast-iron case for not including the transparency in your portfolio.

However, 35mm cannot compete with large-format in its ability to resolve fine detail and nuances of texture and light. The landscape photographer, for example, will find that his pictures have to compete in the market-place with a plethora of 5 × 4in imagery. If you were in the picture-buying business, which format would *you* be more likely to choose?

But 35mm has many applications for which larger formats are inappropriate: action, sports, street photography, candids, informal portraiture, wildlife, reportage, etc. For these subjects, and others, 35mm is the norm. With care 35mm cameras can be hand-held,

An example of a picture that's 'made' rather than just 'taken'. In this motley collection of beach huts huddled beneath a gaunt house, the photographer has seen the potential for a graphic and powerful image. That potential has been realised by the use of a telephoto lens, which tends to compress the elements of a picture into what appears to be a single plane. So here the beach huts seemed to be stacked on top of each other, when there was actually quite a distance between foreground and background.

The slightly sinister mood of the picture has been further emphasised by a prominent grain pattern, particularly in the sky, and by increasing contrast during printing. Pictures like this are the result of choosing the appropriate combination of equipment — camera, lens, filter, film, developer and printing paper — and knowing exactly how the final print will look *before* the shutter is pressed. (Photograph: William Cheung) even with telephoto lenses, allowing the photographer to follow fast-moving subjects with comparative ease. Documentary and reportage photographers can react almost instinctively to rapidly changing situations where speed is of the essence. The difference may be between getting an acceptable photograph and not getting one at all; *that's* where 35mm scores over all other formats.

Compact Cameras

The great advantage of the SLR camera is interchangeability of lenses, but a new generation of compact 35mm cameras offers yet another handy string to a photographer's bow. Some are little more than toys, with film speed settings that preclude the use of anything other than colour print films, and automatic operation that defies any creative intervention on behalf of the user. But most manufacturers offer at least one model with manual or semi-automatic operation, and fixed lenses that will deliver pin-sharp results. Prices for some are on a par with an SLR and standard lens, but a top-quality compact is well worth considering. It takes up minimum space in a gadget bag, and some of the best are diminutive enough to slip into even a shirt pocket.

Compact cameras typically have fixed lenses of 40mm (or thereabouts) which naturally limits their capabilities. They come into their own as back-ups to a more comprehensive SLR outfit; for grab-shots they are ideal.

A basic 35mm camera outfit is within the reach of most photographic enthusiasts. The sheer volume of sales ensures, too, that 'add-on' accessories and appropriate darkroom equipment will be reasonably priced. But things are a little different if you decide to move up-format — to roll-film or 5 × 4in.

Medium-format is the all-purpose term for cameras which use roll-film. The standard format is square, 6 × 6cm, with other cameras offering 6 × 4.5cm and 6 × 7cm negatives. All offer significant advantages over 35mm in terms of image size and resulting quality: an advantage that's obvious as soon as you begin to look at transparencies from both formats on a light-box. When it comes to a straight choice, most picture editors will opt for the larger image.

The 6 × 6cm format is a tried and tested one, and yet few pictures are actually reproduced square: cropping is usually required. The 6 × 4.5cm cameras offer a useful rectangular format and a greater number of exposures per roll. Excellent new cameras are also removing an unwarranted 'amateur' stigma from this format.

A tripod is a piece of equipment that is ignored by too many photographers. It may not have the glamour of a shiny new camera or lens, but it opens up a host of possibilities. The photographer can use the slowest films, the longest lenses, the smallest apertures and the most extended shutter speeds — while making camera-shake a thing of the past. Compositions can be fine-tuned, horizons will be perfectly horizontal and focus (even with budget lenses) will be satisfyingly crisp. In terms of improving technical quality, there can be few better ways of spending spare cash than buying a tripod.

A sturdy support is a useful aid; for some pictures it is indispensable. Here, the photographer has contrasted the static rocks and branches with the sinuous flow of water. A tripod has allowed a slow shutter speed to be used, thus rendering the water as an impressionistic blur. (Photograph: Malc Birkitt)

Wide-angle lenses are almost the standard optics for much landscape and reportage work. But they have another use in helping to open up confined spaces, such as the narrow gangway of this battery hen shed. The broad angle of view allows a great deal of information to be recorded, and the steep perspective both emphasises depth and guides the eye directly to the central figure. The light coming from behind the figure illuminates what would otherwise have been a rather murky scene.

While the aspiring freelance can take on many assignments with the minimum of equipment, it would be foolhardy to venture out without a wide-angle and telephoto to supplement the standard lens. Now, with considerable advances in lens design and specification, there are 'all-purpose' zoom lenses which can virtually take the place of all three. (Photograph: John Russell)

The 6 × 7cm format is commonly known as the 'ideal format', and with good reason. It produces an impressively large transparency which often requires little cropping for acceptable reproduction. The full quality of the original is thus maintained. Roll-film transparencies are far easier to handle and view than 35mm — which is more than can be said for the cameras themselves.

Expense

Most medium-format camera systems require a daunting financial outlay. A camera body and, say, a standard lens is just the beginning of the story. A prism viewfinder to give eye-level — rather than waist-level — operation is almost a must. Then you may want some interchangeable backs, so you can swap film stocks in mid-roll. Filters for the larger lenses can prove pricey, and the lenses themselves can burn a large hole in the wallet. Your current lightweight tripod may not be able to support the extra weight.

Darkroom procedures don't require too much updating if you move to medium format, as long as your enlarger can accommodate the larger negatives. The range of roll-films available is not as wide as for 35mm, though the announcement of roll-film Kodachrome last year met a long-felt need.

If you're not sure whether you can afford a medium-format outfit . . . then you probably can't! One way to move up-format cheaply, and avoid the electrical and optical complications of an SLR, is to invest in a TLR: a twin-lens reflex camera. You get the benefits of the larger format in a sturdy if cumbersome package. Most TLRs have fixed lenses; the models from Mamiya are the only ones that take interchangeable lenses. A second-hand, fixed-lens TLR could set you up in medium-format photography for less than £100; if you find it doesn't suit you then you are unlikely to lose money if you resell it.

Working methods become very different when you decide on large-format: a term that is generally used to cover a negative size from 5 × 4in to 10 × 8in, or larger. The cameras themselves are expensive enough but, like buying a sports car, it can be the running costs that prove prohibitive. Sheet film can be as pricey per shot as 35mm is per roll! The antiquated appearance and mechanical operation of large-format cameras do have one benefit: they demand the highest level of excellence on behalf of the photographer. You just can't afford to press the shutter until the image in the viewfinder is exactly as you want it. Depending on the way you look at it, that can be either a boon or a drawback!

New 5 × 4in enlargers are as expensive and antiquated as the cameras, though examples can often be picked up second-hand for a song. Expect to shell out, too, on accessories such as a deep tank and a giant enlarging easel. There's no point, after all, in getting a 5 × 4in camera just for knocking out 10 × 8in prints.

For most freelance purposes the 5 × 4in format is photographic overkill. Unless your photographs are likely to grace the advertising hoardings that clutter our cities, then a large-format camera could prove a cumbersome and expensive luxury. For most editorial purposes, 35mm or roll-film cameras are perfectly serviceable.

Lastly, it seems a universal human failing to be dissatisfied with what we already have, and to yearn for something better. In photographic terms 'something better' may be a more fashionable camera, an extra body, a longer lens, a more powerful flash-gun . . . These yearnings don't disappear, but they do tend to become less obsessive as a true interest in photography takes over from the urge to accumulate more and more matt-black hardware.

Many photographic commissions can be shot successfully with a basic 35mm camera and standard lens. Add a wide-angle and a short telephoto and you have an impressive armoury — in fact, if not in the eyes of a photographer who has more accessories than creative ideas.

Films

Photographic standards would improve dramatically if photographers agonised a little more about the film they used, and a little less about the dubious 'features' of whatever camera they are currently lusting after. No picture buyer will need to know what piece of equipment was used to produce a particular picture, just as no one will quiz an author about the kind of typewriter he uses!

There is a bewildering variety of films available for all camera formats, and it's vital for the freelance photographer to try out as many as possible, before coming to a considered conclusion about which films are best suited to his own needs.

There are three basic types of film: colour transparency, colour print and black and white print. Colour print film is the staple of the snap-shooter who uses his camera for family occasions and finds that Christmas seems to appear on the beginning and end of every roll.

The great majority of photographs taken are on colour print film; massive sales make both film and processing remarkably cheap. Processing houses fall over each other to grab their share of the valuable printing and processing market. Free films, extra-large prints, one-hour turn-around and free picture wallets are just some of the ploys dreamed up by the gaudily-painted high-street processors.

As prices fall, however, so does quality, and the standard of budget colour printing ranges from the adequate to the downright appalling. Considering how much money gets invested in cameras and lenses, it's amazing that so many hobbyist photographers are content with a sheaf of washed-out prints that look as if they've been developed in chicken gravy.

Colour prints have a limited usefulness to photographers with any realistic pretensions of selling work for eventual reproduction.

There is no such thing as a universal film, and every photographer should experiment with various emulsions before settling on those which best suit his own style and subject matter. The freelance is likely to need a slow and a fast film in both monochrome and colour materials, with a trusted colour negative film for the social photographer whose end-product is colour prints for his clients.

To be prepared for every possible eventuality a freelance needs at least two camera bodies and a range of films always to hand. The choice of film is more difficult when carrying only one camera. A fast black and white film will yield usable pictures in most situations, though the photographer is then left with glorious monochrome. Hand-tinting apart, mono cannot be transformed into colour, but publishable black and white prints can be made from both colour transparency and negative films. This shot is from a colour slide original, transferred to black and white by using a slide-copying device. (Photograph: Mick Rouse)

The problem lies not so much with the films—many are excellent—but with processing and printing. High-street printing houses are geared to mass production: automated printing based on an 'average' negative and the production of postcard-sized prints. Negatives that deviate from the norm will flummox the system. So-called 'creative effects', such as coloured or graduated filters, will give disappointing results.

Colour print films do have applications: such as in social, portrait and wedding photography, where the end-product is a print that will not need to be reproduced or published. But in all these cases print quality should be better than any mass-market processing shop can provide.

The option is for the photographer to make his own prints, or farm the work out to a professional processor. Machine printing can be quite reasonable in both price and quality. Negatives can also be hand-printed: a good deal more expensive, though the extra cost may well be justified in terms of colour rendition (especially skin tones), correct interpretations of special effects and a cropping that is different from the full area of the negative.

It *is* possible to reproduce directly from good-quality colour prints, though the basic currency of the publishing industry is colour transparency film. There are many types, each with their own individual character. It is impossible to give an unqualified recommendation for any emulsion, since they all have their strengths and weaknesses.

The making of a colour film is, to a certain degree, a matter of compromise. The film has yet to be made which delivers a totally accurate rendition of all the colours in any given composition. Every film delivers merely an approximation, however close, of what's 'out there'; it's a matter of personal preference as to which one gives the most aesthetically pleasing result. A film which delivers pleasantly warm skin tones may be less than perfect with the natural colours in the landscape. It's not a matter of right or wrong colour, more a matter of 'horses for courses'.

Reproduction

Personal preference may play a part in finding the most appropriate film for the job in hand, but the reprographic industry has its own quality control. For reproduction, transparencies have to be scanned to produce colour separations. Since every film reacts differently, there is a certain standardisation to ensure consistently good separations for the printer.

For 35mm, Kodachrome is that standard, with Fuji 50 not far behind. For roll-film, Ektachrome gets the nod, though the introduction of 120 Kodachrome may see a change here. This is not to say that other films cannot be reproduced properly, merely that you will not go far wrong with those mentioned above. Picture libraries — again with reproduction practices firmly in mind — often specify Kodachrome for 35mm submissions. Magazines with a reputation for fine photography may have a similar preference for certain film stocks, though most other publications will not be so choosey.

Film speed is an important consideration, and one that needs to be reassessed for every job and every subject. For pin-sharpness Kodachrome 25 is generally reckoned to be the finest 35mm film available. Going up one stop or so in film speed are Fuji 50 and Kodachrome 64. These films offer excellent colour rendition, an almost undetectable grain structure and fine definition of detail: important considerations when technical quality is paramount.

There are occasions, however, when low light or fast-moving action preclude the use of slow films. Increases in speed (200ASA, 400ASA and beyond) produce a corresponding increase in grain and lowering of contrast. Transparency films are now available with a normal speed rating of 1,600ASA, and which can even be 'pushed' a stop or two further when necessary. Ever faster emulsions will no doubt be available shortly.

This search for ever faster and more responsive emulsions in no way undermines the virtues of slower films. The hobbyist photographer may take to ultra-fast films because they save him the effort of carrying a tripod, just as the introduction of wide-to-telephoto zoom lenses may save him the task of switching from one lens to another. But it should be assumed that the freelance is more concerned with quality than convenience, and will take greater pains to produce publishable work.

The advice still stands to use the slowest film compatible with getting sharp results in any given situations. Load faster films only when this is impossible, such as at indoor sports events or where the use of flashguns is prohibited.

Grain for effect

There are now more uses for faster films, however, than merely compensating for low light and difficult shooting conditions. While the vast majority of published pictures have been shot with fine grain and definition firmly in mind, there are times when apparent vices can be turned into virtues. Grain can be emphasised to creative effect, especially when a romantic, nostalgic or dreamy mood is sought. Excessive grain combined with a judicious use of effects filters can produce results that are literally fantastic.

For the grainy effect to work effectively it should look deliberate, and not merely the result of using the 'wrong' film. Detail will be sacrificed in emphasising mood, so grainy pictures work best if the composition is kept very simple. Pictures with grain as big as golf-

The great film-format debate is one of photography's more enduring topics. The users of 35mm, roll-film and large-format cameras will suggest a hundred and one reasons why *their* equipment is the most practical. But it's actually a matter of 'horses for courses', with the best advice being to use the largest format commensurate with getting good results. A 5 × 4in camera is an unwieldy beast, unsuited to rapidly changing conditions, but it comes into its own for capturing subtle nuances of colour, tone and detail in the landscape.

With his camera mounted on a tripod the landscape photographer is able to capture the 'from here to eternity' depth of field that draws the viewer's eyes into the picture. Foreground details help to recreate the sense of space and distance, to produce a balanced composition. (Photograph: R. Alison)

balls have had a vogue lately, particularly in advertising photography, though they have limited uses in editorial photography.

There is another fork in the road to negotiate when choosing a colour transparency film. Some, Kodachrome for example, are 'process-paid': ie, the selling price includes processing, mounting and return by one of the film manufacturer's own laboratories. This means that the photographer will have to wait a few days to see his pictures; at peak times (when the lab is inundated with holiday photographs) that might be as long as a fortnight. Some photographers will find this delay acceptable; others, with pressing deadlines, will look elsewhere for their film stocks. The professional

141

version of Kodachrome offers a faster turn-around in processing.

The majority of transparency films are, in fact, non-process-paid. The user can take these films to the processing house of his choice, or do the job himself. Some labs (particularly in London and other major cities) now offer a same-day processing service, and even a 'we never close' policy. Photographers in a hurry are able to shoot late into the evening and still have the results on a client's light-box early next morning. Professional labs will be able to process to the photographer's precise instructions — though a premium is often charged—which means, for example, that uprated films can receive appropriate development.

There are many processors to choose from; when you find one that provides good service and quality, then stick to it. This is one area when advice can usefully be sought from other photographers. If you have spent weeks in foreign climes shooting pictures you will naturally want your precious films to get the very best treatment. A slipshod processor can wreck weeks of hard work and ruin unrepeatable pictures.

The law is decidedly uncommittal about a laboratory's liability for damage during the processing procedure. If your transparencies of the family pet are unaccountably embellished with scratches or blue spots you may be happy to accept a new film as compensation. But a professional assignment is likely to be a different matter; your loss may total hundreds — even thousands — of pounds. In such circumstances it may be prudent to have films processed in batches, instead of all together.

To muddy the waters further in the matter of choosing transparency films, some emulsions are produced in 'standard' and 'professional' varieties. The professional forms offer accurate, batch-tested speed ratings and a strict consistency in colour rendition. These films are refrigerated to arrest their ageing process, and should be chilled when bought. Professional films should be kept refrigerated until a few hours before use, and then processed promptly. Most photographers find, however, that regular film stocks are more than adequate for their needs.

Transparencies are normally preferred to prints for ease of reproduction, though those photographers accustomed to colour print films may initially be frustrated by the difficulty of viewing transparencies, and their susceptibility to damage. It takes some courage to consign an unrepeatable transparency to the vagaries of the postal system. Fortunately, there are a couple of ways in which transparency images can be copied.

Prints can be made from slides using processes such as

A number of films — both black and white and colour — can be 'pushed': ie rated at a higher ASA number than is normal, underexposed when shooting and then subjected to longer development times. Uprating a film in this way may be the only option in situations with low light levels, but there are disadvantages associated with push-processing. Contrast and grain are increased — often to an unacceptable level.

With an experienced photographer, however, apparent vices can be transformed into virtues. Here, a seascape has been rendered as an atmospheric pattern of grainy dots by pushing film almost to the limits of its tolerance. Push-processing works best with fast films: those nominally rated at 400 ASA or higher. Pushing by one stop will produce a rating of ASA 800. For a more exaggerated effect, as in this picture, films can be pushed as far as ASA 6,400 — a further three stops. (Photograph: John Russell)

Cibachrome chemicals and paper. Print for print this can work out as quite an expensive process, but results from a good transparency can be stunning, with the full detail and colour saturation of the original shining through the print. Most slide-to-print processes can be undertaken at home with the aid of a light-tight processing drum, water-bath for maintaining chemicals at critical temperatures and, of course, an enlarger with a colour head.

The second copying option is to produce duplicate slides from an original. Slide-to-slide duping is a service that most professional labs are happy to perform; prices come down dramatically if a number of duplicates are wanted from a single slide. It's also a job that the photographer can tackle himself. A number of manufacturers produce slide-copying devices which attach to a camera body and hold the slide to be copied perfectly still and straight in relation to the camera.

More expensive duplicating machines offer contrast reduction, cropping and significant alterations to colour balance. Transparencies are already high in contrast, and duping with standard films will merely increase contrast. Purpose-made duplicating films are low in contrast, and will give more acceptable results.

Black and White

It's one of photography's anomalies that black and white prints cost more to produce, in time and cash, than the same pictures shot as colour transparencies. Despite this fact, black and white shots have less earning potential. It does seem unfair, but it's just one more fact of photographic life. There is, nonetheless, a good demand for black and white pictures in markets such as magazines, trade journals and books. Few picture libraries handle black and white pictures these days; the rates of pay do not encourage the stockpiling of easily damaged prints.

There are many black and white films to choose from. They have their own characteristics, which can be exaggerated or negated, depending on the developer and printing paper used. Experimentation is the name of the game, though some help may be given by the comparative tests that the photographic magazines run at regular intervals. Other photographers, too, will have their own favourite films and brews which they will be happy to recommend.

Slow films, such as Pan F at 50ASA or Panatomic-X at 32ASA, deliver biting detail and minimal grain for those occasions when image quality is of prime importance. Medium-speed films, such as Ilford FP4 at 125ASA, offer a versatile compromise between speed and definition. They are the best bet to load up for general photography, where a wide variety of lighting conditions may be encountered.

For low light or action photography turn to old favourites such as Ilford HP5 or Kodak's Plus-X Pan—both rated at 400ASA— which take well to further 'pushing' (ASA 800 or 1600, for example) with a corresponding increase in development times. Grain and contrast will be increased by push-processing, and much detail will disappear into the shadows, but it may make the significant difference between getting a usable photograph and coming home empty-handed. Kodak's new T-Max films are worth trying, the 400ASA version producing results on a par with FP4 film.

Ilford XP1 is something of a maverick among film emulsions. Its introduction was made possible by technological breakthroughs in the manufacture of colour films; it offers the black and white photographer unrivalled latitude in speed, exposure and development times. It's not the universal panacea for all photographic ills, but it comes close. It's an ideal and forgiving film for photographers who tackle a wide range of subjects, and delivers print quality that belies its nominal rating of 400ASA.

A couple of other, more specialised, black and white films deserve a mention. Infra-red film, available from Kodak in the 35mm format, records light rays beyond the visible spectrum. The results are decidedly other-worldly. When the film is used with a deep-red filter, growing foliage is rendered pale and glowing, while blue skies go almost black as a dramatic contrast to white clouds. Infra-red film has applications in surveillance and aerial photography, but the creative photographer will be able to use its eccentric characteristics for more pictorial purposes.

Black and white reversal film (such as Agfa's Dia Direct) produces monochrome slides. One of it's most useful applications is copying black and white prints; the resulting slides will be cheaper and easier to post to prospective clients than a large sheaf of prints.

Films from major manufacturers such as Kodak, Ilford, Agfa, Fuji and 3M will cover every situation likely to be encountered by the freelance photographer. Film will prove to be a major outlay, but there *are* ways to keep costs down. Settling on one or two film types will allow them to be bought in bulk — at a discount — and then stored in a fridge until needed.

The most popular films are also available in bulk lengths. The photographer fills his own cassettes — a task made easier by using a handy gadget called a bulk loader. 'Rolling your own' can represent significant savings as compared to buying boxed films, though care has to be taken during the procedure, as it's very easy for film to be scratched.

Keeping Records

However proficient your photography there's one aspect of freelancing that you've got to get grips with: organisation. For example, it doesn't take long to accumulate boxes of slides and piles of negatives, making it very difficult to locate a particular image in a hurry. Searching randomly through a collection of transparencies is a time-wasting and frustrating business. A system of storage and indexing is vital — and the sooner you adopt one the easier your work will be.

Marketing your own pictures brings a new set of problems. Pictures will be winging their way to and from picture editors; commissions will be negotiated and undertaken; transparencies will be lodged with picture libraries; prints will be awaiting publication in magazines. Your first few successful commissions will be etched firmly in the memory, but after a dozen your memory will start playing tricks. Which magazine did you send a particular set of pictures to? Did you get the pay cheque for a job you did three months ago? How long has it been since you submitted your transparencies to a library?

You will need to develop a suitable way of keeping track of everything you do — every business letter sent out, every submission, every assignment undertaken. You will need to record the dates of submission, of acceptance (or rejection), of publication and of payment. *You* will need these details to operate your business efficiently, while the taxman will develop an interest in the income your photography earns.

But you will have to spend money to earn money, and your legitimate business expenses can be set against tax. Costs of film, processing, travel, printing, stationery, etc should be recorded and corroborated, whenever possible, with receipts and invoices. If you have a darkroom, studio or office in your home then a certain proportion of your domestic bills — gas, electric, telephone, etc — can also be set off against your annual tax demand.

Photography requires great attention to detail and a perfectionist's eye for technical quality. It's vital to bring the same attention to the business side of photography: methodical records and bookkeeping will reduce the time you spend on paperwork and allow you to get on with what you do best — taking pictures.

Photographic materials are notoriously vulnerable to damage. Transparencies begin to fade as soon as they are processed, and they have a finite life-span. You can maximise the useful life of your slides by careful storage and by choice of film stock. Many types of colour prints are even more susceptible to fading, and direct sunlight can diminish their sparkle in a very few weeks.

Negatives are vulnerable principally because they need to be handled during the printing process, and every handling provides an opportunity to become scratched or marked. They must be stored in a way that makes such damage less likely. Black and white prints offer the greatest chance that your photographs will still be seen and enjoyed at their best in the years to come. Archival processing and storage might seem a less than riveting subject to consider, but sooner or later you'll begin to wonder just how long your photographs are going to last.

Storing Negatives

In black and white photography, negatives are your most important asset. Cameras, lenses and prints can always be replaced; negatives, on the other hand, are unique. They deserve the best protection you can offer. Fortunately this is a cheap and simple matter. A 36-exposure roll of 35mm film can be cut into strips, with each strip containing six images. This is a convenient length for handling while printing, and will also slide neatly into the pockets of a negative filing sheet. These sheets normally have seven — not six — pockets; you will appreciate the value of this if you manage to squeeze more than 36 shots out of each film.

The pre-punched sheets fit neatly into a standard ring binder; stored like this your precious negatives will come to little harm. The trouble starts when you want to find a particular negative in a hurry. It's an irksome task to peer at sheet after sheet of negatives. A good method is simply to mount a contact sheet along with every sheet of negatives in the ring binder. It's a lot easier to scan contact prints rather than negatives.

The easiest way to organise your negative collection is to store

them chronologically, without regard for subject matter. Just add negative and contact sheets as soon as possible after processing. Classification can then be achieved with a card index, listing subjects shot and where in your negative file you can find them.

For this system to work, every one of your negatives needs a number to identify it. Instead of marking the negatives themselves you can number the contact sheets. Giving every negative its unique number serves two purposes: ease of retrieval via your card index system and as a convenient label when monitoring the comings and goings of prints.

Exactly how you number your negatives is up to you, but here are suggestions. If you number each strip of six negatives consecutively, then each of the six negatives on each strip can be identified by the letters A – F. Thus negative number 365A would be the first negative on the strip marked 365. A further help could be to add the number of the negative file itself.

Instead of hunting frantically through your negative collection you can consult your card index. Remember to keep it up to date with the salient details of each film you shoot. The subjects listed on each card can be as general or specific as you like. One card, for example, might have the heading of ZOOS, with a 'sub-menu' of particular locations, each with their own negative number.

If this all seems like a lot of trouble, then just wait till you have a few thousand negatives on file, and need to find one in a hurry. Time spent now in organising your files will save a great deal more time — and patience — at a later date.

Transparencies

This system works with negatives because they are essentially an

Filing is one of those essential jobs that most of us find an excuse for not doing. But it saves time, in the long term, to keep comprehensive records on every aspect of freelance photography. And it's vital to create some workable system for storing and retrieving images, so that any particular slide, print or negative can be located in a matter of seconds. There is no one system to suit all photographers, but a shoebox full of unclassified negatives is no system at all!

If each negative is filed and given its own individual number, then it's only a matter of moments to write the number on the back of each newly processed print. A sticker with the photographer's name, address and phone number will ensure that pictures which are sent out are returned — eventually. (Photograph: John Russell)

149

unchanging archive. The only time they are likely to be taken out is when prints are needed. If they are replaced immediately in their files then the system of classification is simple enough. Transparencies, on the other hand, have a tendency to roam further afield — at least they do if you want them to earn money for you. At any one time some of your slides are likely to be on picture editors' desks, in your portfolio case, sitting in your files or perhaps in a magazine ready for projection. It's important to keep tabs of their travels and whereabouts; but how?

Firstly, it's pointless classifying second-rate transparencies, so make a habit of pulling the good shots out of every film you get back from the processing lab. The rest — if you are of an unsentimental nature — should be thrown away, or at least filed out of harm's way in a shoe box in the attic. The saleable shots can be numbered discreetly with indelible ink or a tiny sticker.

However, 35mm slides are unprepossessingly diminutive; the card or plastic mount offers very little room for essential information like your name, address and appropriate caption. A number of printers specialise in producing small sticky labels which are useful for adding your name and address; they can be used for slides, prints, parcels, invoices, etc, and are remarkably cheap.

Each slide is unique; unless you go to the expense of duplicating your best shots you will run the risk of irreparable damage each time they are screened for reproduction. At least you can ensure that they are stored safely when they are not being used. The best bet is to use clear plastic sleeves with individual pockets for each slide. The sleeves can be stored in ring binders like your negatives, or better still in a filing cabinet, suspended on metal bars which slip through the top of each sleeve. This ensures that no pressure is put on the transparencies; nor will they fall inadvertently out of their protective pockets. It's then a simple matter to label each sleeve with a different subject.

Prints

Prints are, on the face of it, less vulnerable to wear and tear in that further prints can easily be made. But printing is costly in both money and time — when both commodities could be better used in producing new images. So your top-quality prints need careful handling and storage to prolong their life expectancy. Boxes for printing paper, suitably labelled with their contents, are ideal for storing prints and cost nothing.

If you've gone to the trouble of printing to exacting archival

150

Flash, whether a small portable unit or powerful studio lights, opens up new photographic horizons. Without a flashgun this shot of break dancing would have been an unrecognisable blur, since the dancer was moving at speed. For portraiture the worst possible place for a flashgun is generally where the camera manufacturers position the hot-shoe: atop the camera pentaprism, on the lens axis. One result of using direct, on-camera flash is the dreaded 'red-eye' effect, which makes people look like extras from a Hammer horror film!

Another result is the casting of harsh shadows, which is equally unflattering in portraiture. A softer light can be obtained by taking the flashgun off the camera and bouncing the reflections off a convenient wall, ceiling or portable diffuser. For this shot, with the photographer lying on the floor, there was no option but to use direct flash and hope for the best.

standards, then don't undo all your good work by poor storage. A number of specialist suppliers sell suitable acid-free mounting boards, tape and boxes.

Make a habit of writing the appropriate negative number on the back of each print. This makes it simple if you need to reprint, and supplies a handy code when making a note of which prints have been sent where. Take care when writing on the back of prints. Ball-point pens, for example, leave grooves in the paper that will show through to the image side. Sticky labels are better. Captions, when required, can be written on paper slips and attached (along one short side only) to the back of each print.

These ideas represent just a few ways in which you can organise your existing photography effectively. You have to decide on a method that suits you, and stick to it. Don't over-complicate the matter.

Much the same applies to the records you keep. Whenever you submit pictures, or even write to a potential client such as a magazine or photo library, you should note down all relevant details. Doing this in a substantial notebook will allow you to keep these records up to date with dates of publication, payment and subsequent return of your work. It's important to know where your pictures have been sent; if a client is tardy about making a decision about whether to use your work then you will know the exact date they were sent, and thus when to prompt the client into making his mind up.

Comprehensive records will preclude the possibility that the same images are submitted to rival publications, with all the problems this course of action can bring about. You will be able to see, at a glance, your rejections and acceptances: the current 'state of play' in your new business venture.

Marketing your own work is time-consuming: even such matters as captioning pictures, writing letters, making phone calls, packing up parcels and sticking on stamps will take up valuable hours. By keeping your records and working methods simple and efficient, your energies can be targeted more effectively towards generating new commissions.

Working from Home

If you plan to combine freelance photography with a nine-to-five job, then it's important to keep photographic costs to a minimum. Otherwise you will soon find that what was planned to be a paying hobby turns out to be a financial liability. It can take some time before your efforts are rewarded by genuine profit, especially if you have had to invest hard-earned cash in new photographic hardware.

You may be sufficiently interested in portraiture or still life to consider setting up a studio. But think again: if you only use a studio in the evenings and at weekends then the cost of renting — or even buying — premises will be prohibitively high when set against potential income. Spare cash is better spent running film through your camera, instead of being tied up in premises or equipment that you don't really need.

Unless your home circumstances are particularly cramped, you need look no further for a base from which to start freelancing. You may decide you need an office, a studio and a darkroom. But the office need be no more elaborate than a desk, a phone and a filing cabinet. The studio can be the living room or spare bedroom, once a few items of furniture have been shifted. And a darkroom can be sited in a walk-in cupboard, or set up when needed in a kitchen or bathroom. You can, in short, take on freelance photographic work with minimal disturbance to everyday family life.

Make a realistic assessment of your needs. Super-wide and long telephoto lenses may be on your shopping list, but on how many occasions will you actually need to use such specialised optics? For those few eventualities it may be more convenient to hire the appropriate hardware by the day. Studios can be found in most towns, if you require the full facilities that they offer. For most of your indoor photography, however — portraiture, table-top work, still life, etc — a suitable space can usually be found in the home.

A Home Studio

Photography is a subtractive medium: what you leave out of a picture is almost as important as what you include. So no one is to know that your portraits have been shot in the front room, unless your pictures hint as much. A makeshift studio might be no more than a plain wall against which your subjects can be posed, but if patterned wallpaper is to your domestic taste then you will need an alternative backdrop.

The simplest solution is a roll of background paper; when hung from a stand the paper can be unrolled into a seamless backdrop for head and shoulder shots or, if extended along the floor, for full-length or group portraits. These rolls are typically 9ft or 12ft wide; when lengths of the paper become creased or grubby the roll can be cut and a new portion used. Available from professional photographic outlets the rolls come in a great variety of colours and finishes. Two or three rolls would give you the chance to ring the changes with your portrait shots, while not representing any major expenditure.

Few modern homes have rooms that make generously proportioned studio spaces. Successful portraiture often requires lenses longer than standard (ie 50mm on the 35mm format, or 80mm on roll-film) if your subject's features are to be rendered without unflattering foreshortening. This necessitates putting a greater distance between camera and subject. Your subject, too, will probably need to stand well in front of the backdrop to avoid casting too many distracting shadows. These factors can mean that you literally have your back to the wall when shooting: hardly the recipe for a productive portrait session!

What's needed—if space is limited—is a little ingenuity. Space *is* needed around your subject; you may need reflectors or supplementary lighting. But your tripod-mounted camera presents a narrow profile; provided you can get an uninterrupted view you can always shoot through the door of an adjacent room or hallway. This is not an ideal way to shoot, but it's better than nothing.

Lighting is the next item on the agenda, and there are a number of options. Daylight has one major advantage — it's free! It is also surprisingly adaptable, with visual qualities that even the most sophisticated artificial lighting set-up cannot match. For portraiture and still life, natural daylight need not represent second best. Diffusers and reflectors — knocked up cheaply out of household materials — can help direct or soften the lighting satisfactorily.

The main drawback, of course, is that daylight is difficult to control. In winter, for example, there is no usable daylight at all at

A home darkroom is very convenient for the freelance who does a lot of black and white work. No commercial printer or processor can ever produce a print *exactly* as the photographer would want it. And very few black and white prints are produced totally 'straight' — without any darkroom manipulations whatsoever — even if the manipulations add up to nothing more than giving a longer exposure to a wishy-washy sky.

For more complex darkroom techniques, such as this example of tone separation, a darkroom is essential. A permanent set-up allows printing and processing to be undertaken with a minimum of fuss and time-wasting. But a temporary arrangement in, say, kitchen or bathroom is a good deal better than no darkroom at all. While it may be less convenient than a purpose-built room, there is no reason why prints should be of lower quality. And that's what counts. (Photograph: Derek Sayer)

the very time you are likely to need it: in the evenings. And at every time of the year you are very much at the mercy of the British weather, with all its unpredictability.

Artificial Light

The two alternatives to natural light are tungsten lighting and flash. Tungsten lighting provides continuous illumination while flash gives a brief, though powerful, pulse of light. Tungsten is far and away the cheaper option and is well suited to the hobbyist's pocket. The effects of a particular lighting set-up are easy to evaluate; in computer terms 'what you see is what you get'.

The basic tungsten lamp is a bulb set in a reflective metal dish; this can be clipped conveniently to most surfaces or mounted on its own purpose-built tripod. Broad reflectors — often used with a diffusing panel — provide soft illumination, while shallow, bowl-shaped reflectors are used when a harsher and more directional light is required. The reflectors are conveniently interchangeable.

A single tungsten light can be used to good effect, especially if some of the light can be 'thrown back' onto the subject by reflecting panels — which may be nothing more exotic than a bed-sheet or piece of white card. But two lights are a more practical combination, allowing one main light and one fill-in.

For black and white photography the colour temperature of the light source is largely immaterial; for colour work, however, it is a vital consideration. Tungsten lights cast a warm glow which produces an orangey cast on daylight colour films. For certain portrait pictures this cast may be an attractive bonus, but for true colour rendition it is advisable to use films which are specifically balanced for tungsten light. Such films may not be available from the local chemist, but any genuine photographic retailer will oblige. In lieu of using tungsten film it is also possible to load up with daylight film and correct the colour balance with a pale blue filter such as an 80B.

Tungsten lights offer a budget entry into studio photography; the drawbacks are that the light output can only be adjusted by moving the lamps towards or away from the subject, the bulbs give off a good deal of heat (no good for photographing ice-cream!), and the bulbs have a nasty habit of blowing at the most inconvenient moments.

When it comes to adaptability tungsten lights can't (pardon the pun) hold a candle to electronic flash, which is now the standard for most professional photography. From diminutive hot-shoe mounted models to powerful studio units, they share a colour temperature that matches daylight. This means they can be used inside and outdoors with standard daylight-balanced film: a great convenience.

Flash

A flashgun is an almost indispensable item in any photographer's camera bag, but studio flash units are a rather different proposition. To justify the considerable expense of buying a competent system — with a few useful 'add-on' accessories — you would need to make

Studio lighting represents a major outlay of cash; if you don't know whether you really need such a set-up or not . . . then you probably don't! Daylight can provide a diffused light source that's perfect for the more informal type of portraiture. Care should be taken with colour film when mixing light sources, such as tungsten, flash and daylight. The appropriate filter can remove the colour cast from a single light source, but no filter can cope with a variety of colour temperatures.

Black and white photography presents fewer problems: the colour of the light source is less important than its intensity and harshness. In this shot the illumination came from a window to the right. With more contrasty light, a reflector (even just a sheet of white card) can be used to give a more even distribution of light.

considerable use of the equipment. Flash units will cope with virtually every lighting eventuality, but this versatility comes at a considerable price — especially if you add a flash-meter to help sort out exposure values when more than one light source is being used.

While flashguns are generally battery powered, studio units are free-standing and use mains electricity. Photographers accustomed to the continuous light source of tungsten may find studio flash a very different proposition, even though many flash units incorporate a modelling light which at least hints at the way your pictures will appear.

The cheaper models of flash unit are low-powered and short on features; more money will buy flash units that will illuminate large sets and still give you choice of fast or slow film stocks and a wide range of possible apertures. Most units can be switched to half or quarter power, and all can be fitted with diffusers, reflectors, 'barn-doors' and umbrellas for altering the harshness, and even the colour, of the light.

Darkroom

If colour transparency film is your chosen medium you may be able to find a niche in the freelance world without ever dunking your hands into luke-warm developer. But the black and white specialist needs access to a darkroom.

Many photographic clubs and galleries have darkrooms on the premises which can be hired by the hour or used at will by club members. This is fine for occasional forays into developing and printing, but is no long-term solution. Using a communal darkroom is like sharing a kitchen: there always seems to be a pile of washing up to do before you can start cooking! Darkrooms have an almost magical way of filling up with junk, and there's really nothing quite like having your own place. If your darkroom is a mess, at least you have no one to blame but yourself!

A spare bedroom makes an ideal darkroom; a few basic plumbing and carpentry skills will work wonders. The trouble with building a darkroom is that you never really know how best to organise the space available until you've used it for a few weeks, by which time it may be too late to make more than cosmetic changes to the layout.

When planning a darkroom it's a very good idea to look at other photographers' work-spaces. You will pick up a host of useful tips; plus, if they have made mistakes you can make sure you don't repeat those mistakes in your own darkroom.

The room has, firstly, to be divided up into a wet and a dry area. The dry side is for the enlarger and ancillary printing hardware, with some provision for storing printing paper, negative files, etc. The wet side accommodates all the processes in which liquids are involved, such as developing, fixing, toning and washing. The two sides must be kept separate, for reasons of sound printing practice and to keep liquids away from electrical contacts and equipment.

Layout

A time and motion expert would throw his hands up in horror at the way that many darkrooms are laid out. It's important to think of all the various processing procedures, and plan the most effective use of available space. Printing, for example, entails taking a sheet of paper from box or printing safe, making an exposure under the enlarger, moving to the developer, stop-bath, fix and, finally, the water-bath for washing. Since this manoeuvre is likely to be repeated thousands of times it is vital that it is made as convenient as possible. While exercise is beneficial, lengthy strolls in the darkroom can soon become tedious!

There are a number of excellent books on the market which give detailed plans for all sizes and types of darkrooms, so a few general hints will suffice here.

No matter how much care you have taken to ensure crisp focus and no camera-shake when taking pictures, all the good work can be undone at the printing stage by using a second-rate enlarger lens. It's a false economy to use anything but the best lens you can afford. When buying a new enlarger, consider how your photography may develop in future — especially in regard to film formats. It's frustrating to move up to medium-format photography, only to find that your enlarger cannot cope with negatives larger than 35mm.

The columns on many modern enlargers are on the flimsy side. Any slight vibration will be greatly magnified when printing, especially when the enlarger head is positioned towards the top of the column. Vibration will produce unsharp prints. The remedy is to secure the top of the enlarger column to the wall behind. Some enlarger manufacturers make special brackets for this purpose, though a do-it-yourself solution should not prove any difficulty.

Wet hands and electricity make a dangerous combination, even when switching room lights on and off. Standard switches can easily be replaced by pull strings. If the string is taken the full length of the darkroom wall or ceiling, it will be possible to turn the lights on or off from anywhere in the room without risking an electric shock from having wet hands.

Insight: Mike Wilson

Mike Wilson is a bus-driver by profession and a photographer by inclination. Despite the demands of shift-work, and operating from his home, he has built up a profitable sideline in wedding and portrait photography. A studio, a darkroom and an office have been shoe-horned into his compact terraced house: it's a model of organisation and efficiency.

His work is geared to the shooting and processing of colour prints, and he's set himself up with the hardware that enables him to produce top-quality prints simply and quickly. There are plenty of other talented photographers around, professional and semi-professional, so Mike has to price his skills competitively in order to get regular commissions. Profit margins are maintained by keeping his overheads as low as possible and by making sure that the time he has available is spent as effectively as possible.

Mike's studio is a spare bedroom, fitted out with small studio lights and an assortment of background papers. The room is suitable for head-and-shoulder portraits; for anything more ambitious he hires a local photographic studio by the hour. The darkroom is diminutive, yet it contains everything he needs to process and print colour materials. His office is simply a phone (with answering machine connected when he's not at home) and a second-hand word processor which produces good-looking price-lists, letters and invoices.

Mike may work from home, but that doesn't mean that he is any less professional than a photographer who has a high-street studio. Everything, from print quality down to a simple invoice, has to reflect the photographer's abilities. Mike has plenty of pertinent advice for other photographers hoping to make a part-time income from social photography — firstly about buying vital equipment:

'When you start out it's not easy to anticipate exactly what you

160

will need; there is no point in spending money on equipment that will be used seldom, if ever. If I were setting up afresh for portrait and wedding photography, these are the items I would put at the top of my shopping list. I would get a basic 35mm system: one or two camera bodies (no need for top-of-the-line models) and a small selection of lenses — 28mm, standard 50mm, 100mm and a converter would be adequate.

'Then I would get a medium-format system — as comprehensive as I could afford. A 645 outfit is ideal, since you get fifteen shots per roll compared with twelve on the square 6 × 6cm format; that can represent quite a saving on film. Make sure that at least the standard lens for the 645 camera has a leaf shutter, enabling flash to be synchronised at any shutter speed.

'A medium-format camera is perfect for covering weddings; the larger negative gives the quality that people want for their wedding albums. It's also important to establish your credibility when most of the guests will have their own 35mm cameras. Years ago I covered weddings with a very cheap 35mm camera; there would always be other people with their Pentax and Nikon SLRs who would look down on me. Of course, anyone can buy a piano, but that doesn't mean they can play . . .

Home Printing

'I process and print at home, so it's important that my darkroom is both functional and comfortable. My enlarger copes with all formats up to 6 × 7cm, and I have a Durst RCP20 roller-transport processor for colour work. It means that as soon as a print is put into the processor the room lights may be turned on and another print prepared: a great time-saver and so much simpler than messing around with drums and developing dishes.

'Everybody thinks that a colour analyser is essential for colour printing, but an exposure meter is really all I need. More important is a voltage stabiliser for the enlarger, to ensure that prints are of a consistent quality—especially for repeat orders. A stabiliser means I can reprint a photograph with a known filtration and get a print that's identical to one I did months ago. I know the filtrations, and other details, because I log them in a notebook. It may seem like a hassle, but it pays off in the long run.

'My enlarger is not free-standing; it's fixed solidly to the wall, which ensures that vibration never affects print quality. The baseboard is adjustable; it can easily be lowered for making large prints. I recommend using light-tight paper safes. I have five of

them for various papers; just press the lid and a piece of paper is delivered into your hand. That's so much more convenient than fiddling around with envelopes and boxes, plus you can never fog the paper accidentally.

'An extractor fan is essential when working with colour chemicals in a confined space. As a final touch the darkroom has a double layer of carpet: a welcome touch of comfort as I spend many hours standing up in there.

'I use rechargeable NiCad batteries for all my gear; a recharger and a few sets of NiCads save a lot of money over the years — especially if you're in the habit of putting away flashguns without turning them off! A battery tester allows me to check on their condition, so when I go to shoot a wedding I can ensure that I have fully charged batteries for all my equipment. You have to make sure that everything is working properly, as there are already enough stresses and strains in doing wedding photography. It may be raining and blowing a force-ten gale, but it's *you* who'll get the blame if the pictures don't come out well . . .

'I advertise regularly in the local press, though a lot of my work — especially weddings — comes by word of mouth. That's the best form of advertising. If a couple are happy with their wedding pictures then they're likely to give my name to friends and members of their families.'

If you plan to spend much time shooting portraits, then a home studio — however makeshift — will make the task a great deal simpler. And you can be assured of technical excellence to match your ideas by investing in a medium-format camera. The larger negative records much greater detail than 35mm, and the full tonal range to be found in your subject. (Photograph: Malc Birkitt)

Portfolio presentation

'I cannot praise', said John Milton, 'a fugitive and cloistered virtue.' It's certainly true that you gain nothing by keeping your best photographs to yourself; they've got to be seen. Whether you're trying to sell existing work, or getting photographic commissions, you are going to have to subject your photographs to an editor's critical assessment.

You can expect brutal honesty from those in a position to buy and commission photography. They will no doubt see a great many young hopefuls with their portfolio cases; with the number of aspiring photographers around it is definitely a buyer's market. Your submission of photographs has to compete with many others, so you have to present the strongest possible case for an editor to use *you*, rather than somebody else.

Of all the picture editors you're likely to see, the most important one is you. It's your responsibility to ensure that only your best work is seen. You are, after all, judged only by what you release and not what is left in the darkroom bin.

Yet the truth is that we are often the least capable critics of our own work. Every picture we take has both a creative and a nostalgic value. We remember the circumstances under which our pictures were taken: a particularly enjoyable day, perhaps, or in good company. So we ascribe pleasant memories to certain pictures, no matter how poor those pictures might be. Objectivity is a very difficult quality to bring to our photographs.

The opinions of family and friends are equally suspect: a few words of extravagant praise can quickly instil a photographer with an unrealistic appraisal of his own expertise. You may become *the* photographer of the family, but don't let it go to your head! The people close to you are unlikely to give you what you need: a 'warts and all' appraisal of your photography. Picture editors will, after all, have no such scruples about hurting your feelings.

When you want to start selling your pictures there comes a point at which you have to take stock and present your best work in a visually attractive way. The process might as well begin by weeding out all photographs with technical shortcomings. It can be depressing to scrutinise some of your favourite transparencies with a magnifying glass, only to find them spoiled by processing marks, over-exposure or uncritical focus. But it has to be done.

Even such a basic notion as focus can be misunderstood. Virtually every photograph should contain an area of pin-sharp focus. It might be only a small part of the picture (as when a figure stands out sharply against an unfocused background) or it might be the whole scene, such as a landscape shot with a wide-angle lens to give maximum clarity and visual information. Both treatments are valid, provided that the results realise the photographer's intentions.

In the first example above, for example, the figure or portrait should be as sharp as possible, to give maximum definition against a backcloth of blur. A large lens aperture is a useful aid in separating foreground from background, but the narrow band of focus does make critical sharpness more difficult. Conversely, the landscape might be shot on the smallest possible aperture, perhaps at the expense of shutter speed. The result might be very slight camera-shake that renders the picture soft.

'Soft' is a word that you'll hear a lot from the people who will be looking at your work. It's a rather misleading term, because it has nothing to do with the soft-focus effects achieved with diffusion filters. It indicates, instead, a slight deterioration of image quality caused either by camera-shake or incorrect focusing. A 35mm transparency needs only the slightest degree of softness to be unsuitable for enlargement and reproduction. The first time you go through your transparencies with a coldly critical eye is probably the moment you vow to use a tripod more often!

Uncritical focus is a very common fault, because it can easily go unnoticed. Look through your favourite shots: leave those that are soft out of your portfolio, no matter how good the colour and composition might be.

Exposure

Exposure problems are easier to spot, because only a glance is needed to confirm under- or over-exposure. A transparency that's too light is unusable: bin it. Slight under-exposure is preferable, since the colours can be adjusted slightly during the reproduction

process. Under-exposure by a stop, or half a stop, also gives stronger and more saturated colours. Aim for perfect exposure by all means, but if you must err then err on the side of under-exposure — for transparencies at any rate.

Processing faults on transparencies are a constant source of frustration among photographers. It's a subject that crops up in conversation again and again, whenever two or three photographers are gathered together. Some can complain bitterly — for as long as anyone will listen — about the blue spots, colour casts, 'pin-holes' and scratches that always seem to blight their otherwise successful shots.

Some films are bought 'process-paid', ie you pay for the cost of processing when you buy them. Kodachrome, for example, must be processed at one of Kodak's own laboratories. Since Kodachrome is still the accepted standard by which other films are judged, this monopoly of processing puts photographers at the mercy of a single lab. If mystery spots and marks appear on your transparencies (it happens from time to time) there is not a great deal you can do about it, apart from changing film stock and processor. Suffice it to say that if you find an independent processing lab that gives good service without damaging your transparencies then stick with it.

In the short term you will have to exclude all scratched and damaged transparencies from your portfolio, along with those that fail to make the grade through poor exposure and focusing. Your pile of transparencies will probably be a good deal smaller now, and we haven't even looked at the aesthetic qualities yet . . .

Editing Pictures

The visual qualities and failings of your photographs are harder to

There is an element of luck about shooting good action pictures that makes this kind of photography both exciting and exacting. But it's also true that the successful sports photographer can make his own luck by careful pre-planning. The correct choice of lens and film is vital; they have to match the pace of the action, the distance of the photographer from his subject and the prevailing light levels.

It is helpful if the photographer can pick the best vantage points, though in many sports these may be restricted by the event organisers or available only to accredited photographers with the appropriate passes. There are, however, many opportunities for the freelance to build up a portfolio of sports pictures by attending small races and meetings. (Photograph: Martyn Barnwell) gauge. Photographs appeal visually, emotionally and intellectually; there is just no objective yardstick by which to measure them. A photograph which has one picture editor beaming with delight will be rejected out of hand by another expert.

The best you can do is to edit your pictures unsentimentally — asking yourself whether they really achieve what you set out to achieve. A fussy composition, a distracting background, an inappropriate expression, jarring colours — these failings can dilute the visual message you are trying to get across to your audience. If you can't satisfy yourself about the success of a photograph, then it has no place in your portfolio. When in doubt, throw it out.

If you have gone through your transparencies with a fine-tooth comb, then your pile of successful pictures may be dispiritingly small. No matter; you will do yourself no favours by showing second-best pictures. Your portfolio will impress by quality rather than quantity.

The presentation of your work is nearly as important as the pictures themselves. You have to sell your own professionalism as well as your ability to take a snap. Your portfolio is your shop-window; the way it is laid out will speak volumes to the picture editors you see. It should be a continually updated collection of your most stimulating photographs, presented in a form that shows them off to best advantage.

This form will depend on whether your work is primarily prints or slides; fortunately there are a number of presentation aids to buy (or make) that will help you to present a better image.

Let's start with transparencies. In an ideal world they should be viewed on a colour-corrected light-box, or projected onto a screen in a darkened room. All too often, however, they are simply held up to the most convenient light source, whether that be a fluorescent light or a blue sky. So transparencies must be presented so that they can be handled easily, with enough protection to keep them free from accidental damage. Even a greasy thumb-print can be difficult to shift.

The least impressive way to show slides is in the little plastic boxes that processors use for sending them by post. Anyone viewing them has to tip them out, handle each one individually and then stuff them back in the box again. It's a time-consuming and fiddly chore guaranteed to put any picture editor into a jaundiced frame of mind. And every time a slide is handled is one more opportunity for it to be damaged. You've taken a lot of trouble to pick out the winners; if you treat them with more respect then perhaps a picture editor will too.

168

Showing Slides

It's more convenient to view slides *en masse*. A number of suppliers sell sheets of matt-black card which have apertures cut out to accommodate transparencies. All formats are catered for, though this method of presentation is particularly good for 35mm and medium-format transparencies; 5 × 4in transparencies are usually mounted in individual sleeves. Slides slot into holding flanges behind each cut-out hole, allowing the sheet to be viewed on a light-box. The black card also helps to cut down distracting flare from the light source.

The sheets of card are usually sandwiched in an envelope of clear plastic, so that individual slides need not be handled. This form of presentation looks polished and professional: a point that won't go unnoticed by any picture editor. But these mounts do have a drawback: the slides are so well protected that it can be quite a hassle to take them out and put them back in. If the slides are secured to the back of the card mount with sticky tape then the problem gets worse.

Card mounts are acceptable, providing you don't want to chop and change your picture selection too often; they're less acceptable if your potential client wants to remove a few slides and view them together on a light-box. It's quite a reasonable request: to see, for instance, how individual pictures might work together on the printed page.

A more adaptable way of showing slides is in clear plastic sleeves with pockets for individual images. Some have a clear lift-up flap which affords greater protection from dust and careless handling. Others also feature a frosted sheet at the back of the slides which provides a pleasantly diffused illumination on a light-box. For good looks alone, they come second to the black card mounts; on all other counts they come out a clear winner.

Transparent sleeves can be stored in a variety of ways: 'on the road' in a briefcase or box, at home suspended on rods in a filing cabinet. They represent money well spent.

Prints

Photographic prints are viewed in normal room light and require different presentation ideas. Generally speaking, prints are less vulnerable to damage than transparencies. Since the original negatives are safely under lock and key at home, photographers have fewer qualms about their prints being handled. Nevertheless, printing is a time-consuming business and it's wise to present prints in a way that combines ease of viewing with a degree of protection.

A miscellaneous pile of dog-eared prints is an unedifying sight; a picture editor will get the impression that the photographer doesn't care enough about his work to present it properly. The word 'portfolio' implies a certain uniformity of idea and intent; don't dilute the impact of your work by falling at the last hurdle. Instead, the uniformity of your approach should be carried through into your printing methods.

Print to a standard size whenever possible. If you cannot avoid having prints of different shapes and sizes, then it's a good idea to mount them all on identical sheets of card. A stack of mounted prints will fit snugly into a box or portfolio case, and won't rattle around during transit.

There's quite an art in mounting black and white or colour prints. The simplest — and least pleasing — way is simply to glue a photograph to a piece of card. The result will almost certainly look rather amateurish; if you're going to the trouble of mounting prints then you might as well do it right. Right?

A window mat makes a good print look great — well worth the effort.

Window mats win approval from archivists too. If you print to acceptable archival standards and use acid-free board and tape then your prints will still be around when you are long gone. This may not be a pressing concern right now; but if you are serious about your photography then the concept of archival permanence will rear its ugly head at one time or another.

It's a subject that breeds either obsession or apathy. Few photographers think about the keeping qualities of their photographs until their slides and prints start to fade. It's only then they become obsessive.

Mounting Pictures

Window-mounting — whether for presentation or framing — serves many purposes. Prints do not touch one another, nor the plastic sheets in a portfolio case, nor the glass in a frame. To do the job properly you will need a mat-cutter: a device that will provide a neat bevelled edge to your window mount.

For each print you will need two identical sheets of stiff card, best purchased from an artists' supplies shop. Daler, and other companies, make good quality card in a wide variety of colours. Choose an overall size for your mounts that will easily accommodate a variety of print sizes.

Technical excellence is something to which the freelance must aspire, and there should be no room in his portfolio for pictures which fall short on either aesthetic or technical merit. Portfolio pictures should be viewed with a coldly critical eye . . . and a magnifying glass or loupe. It may be disappointing to find that so many favourites are really not quite as sharp as you'd thought, but all such pictures must be unsentimentally discarded.

A portfolio represents the only chance for an inexperienced photographer to impress a picture editor, so a great deal of thought should go into showing work to best advantage. First impressions are important, and a selection of pictures beautifully ordered and mounted will say a lot about the photographer's attitude and professionalism. Care should be taken, too, with print quality; a print isn't 'finished' until it's been spotted with a brush to disguise minor blemishes.

Your print should be taped, at the corners, to one sheet of card. An aperture is cut in the other sheet; it's through this window that the print will be viewed. You can, of course, cut this window with a sharp knife or scalpel blade, but a bevel-edged cutter is better. These gadgets, again available from specialist art shops, come in both cheap and expensive versions. Budget models are simply devices that hold a sharp blade at a 45° angle. More adaptable, and accurate, are larger cutting jigs that allow you to cut bevel edges in quantity without having to rough out the projected cuts in pencil before you start.

The end result — give or take a modicum of skill and a steady hand — will be much the same: a neatly cut mat. The two sheets of card can be hinged together with tape. This sandwich of print and two boards gives your photograph a rigidity that enables it to be viewed with ease.

Another way to present prints is to slip them (mounted or unmounted) into the clear acetate sleeves of a portfolio book. As with slides, the plastic affords your prints protection from careless handling, though 'clear' plastic is by no means as transparent as glass. After much use the plastic can become marked and scuffed — again to the detriment of viewing your pictures. And the plastic sheets reflect the light to an irritating degree. No matter: this is how most photographers show a portfolio of prints.

Prints that are handled repeatedly may be laminated: an irreversible process which heat-seals photographs between clear plastic. The result resembles a glossy restaurant menu and repels all possible damage, short of launching an attack with a pair of scissors. This is a specialised service, now being offered by many professional processing houses.

The ideas above cover the most usual ways of presenting a representative body of work to a potential buyer of your photography. But there are a few other criteria to consider and the next chapter will concentrate on the personal approach: how to present *yourself* as well as your pictures in the best possible light.

Presenting a Better Image

However good your photographs may be, you have to take pains to show your work to picture buyers. Don't expect them to beat a path to your door. Things will only happen if *you* make them happen. Reticence will only leave the way open to more strident — and probably less-talented — self-publicists.

You need what the Americans call a 'game plan': an understanding of your own skills and deficiencies and a firm idea of what you want to do. You must decide, for example, whether you wish to sell existing work or chase after commissions. Do you exploit a speciality or try to be a jack of all trades? Do you approach magazines with new ideas, or do you distance yourself from self-promotion by dealing with a picture library? Do you want to keep your photography as a sideline, a profitable hobby? Or do you harbour realistic hopes of one day taking up photography full-time?

Only you can make these decisions — with a little advice, perhaps, from people with more experience of the photography business. It is vital to differentiate between those areas of the communications industry that are open to part-timers and those that rely wholly upon trained professionals.

You are unlikely, without a recognised track record, to be offered commissions in advertising photography, where both budgets and expectations will be high. The opportunities detailed in this book provide more realistic opportunities for talented but unproven photographers. Aim high, by all means, but temper your ambition with realism. And don't be put off by early disappointments; most successful practitioners in the creative arts have suffered the trauma of rejection, only to bounce back and redouble their efforts.

If you have yet to sell any of your photographic work, then the publishing world has been operating successfully without you up to now. You have to make a valid case for people to use your work.

Almost as important as the photographs themselves is your attitude — to photography, to the people you are dealing with and to the prospect of getting work.

High-pressure salesmanship, for example, is liable to alienate potential clients. You are selling your skills, not a set of encyclopaedias. Diffidence, too, will win few friends; if you are enthusiastic about your portfolio then you will find your enthusiasm may be infectious.

To an outsider looking in, the world of publishing can appear somewhat glamorous. The truth is rather different: editorial staff have to work to punishing deadlines and the glamour is mostly illusion. There's little time for quaffing champagne when there's a magazine issue to get out! Nevertheless, there isn't an editor in the land who will pass up the opportunity to see a new photographer's work, since the magazine market relies heavily on outside contributors to complement in-house writers and photographers.

Showing your Portfolio

So you want to show your work to a magazine editor, but don't know how to go about it. Your options are to take your portfolio along in person, or send a submission of pictures by post. Despite the time and expense involved, the former option is always the most instructive. For a few minutes you will have the undivided attention of a member of the editorial staff. You will be able to put faces to familiar names and get to know exactly what the requirements of the magazine are.

It's impossible to overestimate the importance of the personal approach. Magazine photography relies largely on mutual trust between an editor and his contributors, and a handshake is more common than a written contract. It's not good business practice for an editor to commission work from a photographer he's never met; deadlines have to be met and editors don't want to waste their time chasing up recalcitrant freelancers who can't get their work in on time.

Go to see editors you think might be interested in your work, but *never* turn up unannounced. Always make an appointment, by letter or phone. Saying 'I was in the area and thought I'd pop in' is both unprofessional and unproductive; it will mark you as an inconsiderate time-waster and ensure that the editor will immediately develop a rather jaundiced impression of you and your work.

Magazines have different methods of seeing photographers. Some

This shot is from a picture story on stock-car and banger racing. Seen in isolation such a picture may seem somewhat confusing, but it makes sense when it appears with other pictures from the series that help to put it into perspective. A portfolio is a bit like a picture story: the choice of pictures, and the order in which they appear, should form a satisfying sequence that best displays the photographer's particular skills.

No two picture buyers have the same requirements, so the best portfolios are those in which the pictures can be changed quickly and conveniently. The potential client should feel, correctly, that the portfolio has been put together especially for *him*.

won't see them at all—asking, instead, that the photographers leave their portfolios at reception. The idea, naturally enough, is that a busy picture editor can go through the portfolio at his own pace, without a photographer breathing down his neck. But it can be dispiriting for a photographer to call back to collect his portfolio, only to read a curt note of rejection. He doesn't know *why* his pictures have been rejected, and has missed out on valuable words of advice or encouragement. There is no guarantee, either, that his work has been seen at all . . .

This method of viewing photographers' portfolios is becoming increasingly common, as more of an editor's time becomes taken up with seeing young photographers. But it does little to help photographers judge the relevance and quality of their pictures. Fortunately, most magazine editors are still prepared to see photographers along with their portfolios.

Back we come to the photographers' attitude, however, and all too often they hinder their own cause; a few examples from personal experience will reinforce the point.

An editor is looking through your portfolio. Do you add a running commentary, or do you let the pictures speak for themselves? The best advice is to speak up when you can add something to the pictures, but there is no point in burbling on manically. Don't, for example, point out defects in your own work. It does happen, but is thoroughly unconstructive. It merely informs an editor that you cannot edit your own work properly.

Don't make excuses, however plausible, about why you couldn't bring your best work along; an editor will get the correct impression that he is being fobbed off with second-best. It's equally pointless to stress how difficult it may have been to take certain shots. It's irrelevant; either the pictures are effective or they're not.

Don't produce hundreds of pictures with an apologetic shrug of the shoulders, saying 'I didn't know what to bring along, so I brought everything'. Nothing is more guaranteed to make a picture editor's heart sink to his boots. It's an easy matter to pick a dozen transparencies out of a selection of fifty, but after scrutinising hundreds of images an editor's critical abilities – not to mention his patience — will be wearing unpromisingly thin!

Don't try to blind an editor with science or pretentious artiness, and don't criticise him — well, not too much — if he makes a selection that doesn't include your own favourite images. *You* may have edited your work with great care, but *he* will have a better understanding of the requirements of his particular publication.

Don't try to pressurise an editor into using your work; if he feels he's on the wrong end of a hard sell, then he's likely to turn you down flat. On the other hand a grovelling approach is just plain embarrassing. Have faith in your work, listen to what an editor has to say and accept a rejection with as much good grace as you can muster in the circumstances.

There are a few other matters of importance to consider when you are showing your portfolio. Magazines are sensitive about their opposition, particularly other periodicals in the same field. It's good sense to tell an editor if you are selling similar — or identical — pictures to a rival magazine; he will appreciate your candour. It's embarrassing for the same picture to turn up in two magazines at the same moment — and a major headache if those pictures happen to occupy the cover. Honesty in these matters is definitely the best policy, and also applies to your ability to take on an offered photographic commission. Don't agree on a restrictive deadline that you won't be able to meet.

Try, as far as possible, to see the editor's point of view as regards the publication of your work. His proposed treatment of the pictures may not coincide with your own ideas. If you place too many strictures and conditions on the use of your pictures, then an editor may begin to feel that you are simply being awkward.

The Personal Touch

There is no substitute for meeting a potential picture-buyer in person. After all, you are not dealing with companies but with individuals. And you are selling yourself almost as much as your pictures. You will be able to discover a picture-buyer's precise requirements in a matter of minutes, and the next time you phone him he will be able to put a face to a name. The more you learn about the people you deal with, the better the chance of forming a worthwhile business relationship.

It's a fact, however, that the communications industry in this country is largely based in and around London. This is where you will find most of the major magazines, book publishers, picture libraries and the ancillary businesses that oil the wheels of the publishing industry. If all roads used to lead to Rome, then most ambitious full-time photographers will gravitate to the capital sooner or later. You only have to stroll around central London to realise that every other person seems to be carrying a portfolio case! Photographers who want to make it in the advertising world, for example, will find a London base almost essential. When art directors, clients, models and stylists need to meet up regularly throughout a shoot, then the venue must be conveniently sited for all concerned.

But this book is aimed at those who want to make *extra* income from their photography, and who are probably holding down full-time jobs quite unconnected with taking pictures. For these people it will probably not be practical to move to London, or even to visit the capital on a regular basis. The skills of these photographers has to be marketed through the mail. It's not an ideal way to sell pictures, but if you live outside London then you may simply have no other realistic option.

It might seem that the telephone should be the best way of introducing yourself to a prospective picture-buyer. Few people,

A photographer's portfolio should contain pictures which speak for themselves, such as this characterful portrait of writer Robert Bolt. The photographer may not, after all, have the opportunity to talk a potential picture buyer through his collection of images. A portfolio should also feature work of a kind that the photographer would like to tackle in the future, in respect of style and subject matter. (Photograph: Stephen Hyde)

however like to be hassled over the phone by someone they don't know. Making initial contact by letter allows you to submit examples of current work and tear-sheets of already published pictures. An editor can look at your work at his ease, and make his own conclusions. Equally likely, of course, is that he will leave your submission languishing in the bottom of his in-tray! It's at this point that a phone call can help: to make sure that your submission is getting due attention.

Keep Up to Date

Let's assume that you have a selection of pictures and an appropriate market to send them to. Don't rely on outdated listings for the address and the person you need to contact. People in the publishing business change jobs regularly; if your letter is addressed to a magazine's last editor but one then you hardly give a favourable impression of being 'on the ball'.

Pare down your picture selection to a number that can be viewed without inducing total boredom in the recipient. If it's an appropriate selection of images you won't have to do anything other than enclose a brief covering letter. You won't need to send a long-winded cv, a résumé of your published credits or a critique of your own pictures. Do remember to enclose a stamped addressed envelope in which your pictures can be returned — sooner or later.

A little consideration about the best way to send your pictures will keep postal costs to a minimum, ensure that your work arrives undamaged, and enable the recipient to view your pictures without breaking his finger-nails getting into an impenetrable package. Good packaging can also be used again when your pictures are returned — important since not everyone will take as good care of your pictures as you do.

Prints are easiest to post if they are printed to a uniform size, and not too large. 10 × 8in prints are perfectly adequate for most purposes; anything over 12 × 16in is visual overkill, and merely pushes up costs of both printing and posting. Find some method of keeping prints from getting damaged in transit; even a crease or dog-ear may render a print unusable. It's asking for trouble to put them in a flimsy envelope; better to sandwich them between sheets of thick card (or even hardboard) before being slipped into a tough manilla envelope or padded Jiffy bag. Transparencies, held in plastic sheets, can be safely posted in a similar way. Glass-mounted slides are best not sent through the post at all; if any of the mounts shatter then some of the transparencies are certain to be damaged.

So much for speculative submissions of existing photography. Ideas for pictures and features should be presented as simply as possible: describe your proposal, enclose examples of your work and a brief covering letter. If a reply isn't forthcoming within a fortnight, phone up and jog the editor's memory about your idea.

Planning Projects

Basic photographic techniques are not hard to learn. If 'good habits' are fostered from the very beginning, then most of us are soon able to turn out pictures of publishable quality. Correct exposure, crisp focus, thoughtful composition and an acceptable print quality: these aspects have to be taken for granted before any realistic foray is made into the freelance jungle.

But proficiency is not enough: the freelance photographer must be a self-starter, able to initiate his own ideas as well as responding to commissioned assignments. The hobbyist photographer has no commercial constraints on his time and energies; he can shoot *what* he wants, *when* he wants. This is fine if his pictures are going no further than the family album, but freelance ambitions require a great deal of self-discipline, organisation and creative input.

Practice makes perfect, or so it's said, and there's a lot that a photographer can do to hone his talents towards a more marketable style. When we start taking photographs we tend to think in terms of single images, whereas a good deal of the work open to freelancers relies on the ability to shoot picture *stories*.

Long before magazines start falling over themselves to hire your talents, you can set photographic tasks for yourself. They will get you into the good habit of covering a story in depth, with a self-imposed deadline. You will learn other skills: writing comprehensive picture captions, editing your work and presenting the results in a form acceptable to a paying client. Perhaps more importantly you will begin to acquire a visual vocabulary. It's not an easy language to learn . . .

Ideas for pictures and stories do not materialise out of thin air; they have to be fostered and developed. While it's a good idea to carry a camera as often as possible, most saleable pictures require a good deal more thought than just wandering the streets waiting for something to happen.

Self-motivation is vital. Magazine editors, picture libraries and other people involved in picture sales will be able to offer valuable guidance about the subjects and styles they are interested in seeing. But a photographer able to generate a constant flow of new ideas is much more likely to get work than one who simply waits for the telephone to ring. A photographer can create his own work by dreaming up his own ideas, setting out a rational proposal and approaching a suitable market. If the idea is good, it will sell.

The people whose job it is to buy and commission photography are busy people. Magazine editors, for example, spend a great deal of their working day on mundane but important matters: dealing with writers, designers, publishers, photographers, printers and readers. It is never easy to find time for the equally important job of forward planning; there are always 101 other more pressing jobs that have to be dealt with.

This means that photographers and writers who can put forward solid proposals for features and articles will be very welcome. So if you have what you think is a worthwhile idea, don't keep it to yourself!

Ideas File

Ideas can come from intensive research or a chance remark overheard in a pub. No matter the source, it's a good idea to translate good picture ideas into black and white. A notebook or system of filing cards will keep track of possible projects, and provide a schedule for using your free hours most profitably and efficiently.

The quickest way to generate a stock of ideas is to leaf through current magazines, particularly those on topics that already interest you. See what kind of pictures are used, and how they relate to the articles and features. You will soon get an idea of each periodical's own picture requirements. There is no point in copying any of the pictures you see, but it's worthwhile to clue into a periodical's basic style.

Many picture libraries are keen to circulate lists of the pictures they are currently seeking on behalf of clients. These lists are bound to throw up a few picture ideas that you will be able to tackle. Pictures of palm-fringed beaches or exotic landmarks may well be impossible to shoot, though a large percentage of wants can be met by photographers willing to research the subjects and, if necessary, set up shots that cannot be found by observation alone.

One good idea may produce pictures for a variety of markets—an

Photographing rock bands is seldom easy; shooting with a telephoto lens from the back of the stalls is downright impossible! A stage-side vantage is preferable, enabling the photographer to use a standard lens (which usually has the widest aperture) or even a wide-angle. If you can shoot your pictures at a rehearsal or sound check, so much the better. Get to know local bands; many will go onto bigger and better things.

There are many magazines which need a good supply of rock pictures — often from shows outside London. What's needed is pictures that offer something a little out of the ordinary: not just endless shots of singers who seem to be impaled on a mike stand. Getting backstage may require little more than a bit of chat, a sense of humour and a promise (keep it!) to give a print or two to the people you photograph. (Photograph: Simon Archer)

important consideration if you need to spend time and money organising a project or trip. You may, for example, know somebody who is a member of a local hang-gliding club, and who is happy to help you get some good action pictures. A day out could give many opportunities for subsequent picture sales. The hang-gliders may be happy to buy a print of themselves floating through the clear blue yonder; and if somebody has been particularly helpful in setting up a shot then a print is always a good way of saying thanks.

Hang-gliding, with its connotations of windswept freedom, might make a good subject for stock photography: colourful hang-gliders against an uncluttered background of sky or fields, or perhaps flying over a local landmark. A variety of pictures could be shot, in both vertical and horizontal croppings, with the gliders occupying both small and large areas of the viewfinder.

The flat light of midday is unlikely to produce the most attractive images. Dawn or dusk will bring a welcome sparkle to colourful sails and clothing. This is, after all, a popular photographic subject, so your pictures must have something extra to stand out from the crowd. If you are blessed with an 'interesting' light (and that doesn't necessarily mean unclouded blue skies) then don't stint on film. On the other hand, shooting roll after roll in heavy drizzle is unlikely to produce pictures that will sell. So put your camera away and plan another day's photography instead.

There may be potential for a picture story. While hang-gliding is now quite a popular sport, there are always a few eccentrics who insist on flying with a dog strapped on next to them, or attempting a long-distance flying record. Any unusual aspect could provide a short picture feature for a general-interest magazine or local paper.

Given a little planning it would also be possible to attach a camera — equipped with ultra wide-angle lens and autowind — directly to a hang-glider frame. A secure clamp and cable release will enable pictures to be taken in flight, often with fascinating results. Any idea that brings new perspectives to a well-photographed subject will increase the chance of the pictures selling.

With a little imagination, almost every situation can provide material for a photographic project. It may be a day's shooting, or a long-term preoccupation. Either way, you will be working out picture ideas and shooting with an end-use in mind: that's always more productive than photographing in a random fashion.

Familiar Subjects

If project ideas are hard to come by, look no further than your own hobby, job or neighbourhood. They may be boringly familiar to you, but there will undoubtedly be some aspect which has picture potential, if only you can look at your surroundings with more than usual objectivity.

Your file of ideas should include more than just a list of possible subjects. How many times do we pass something we'd like to photograph, but find that we have left our camera at home or the light is wrong? Make a note of these locations before they slip from the memory, and details of the best season or time of day to get your shots.

The selling of original photographic prints has, until quite recently, been virtually impossible. People were prepared to pay quite handsomely for etchings, screen-prints and lithographs, but generally baulked at the idea of paying for photography. The situation is changing, however, and a few dozen photographers in this country are supplementing their incomes by selling prints. The publishing of limited editions helps to create a collectors' market and, for better or worse, ensures that original prints can represent a good financial investment.

Those photographers without a household name to bolster print sales may try another medium for their 'fine art' photographs: the burgeoning market for posters and postcards, or what the Americans call 'photo-decor'. Photographic posters give people the chance to decorate their homes with contemporary images without paying a fortune for the privilege. The poster and postcard boom has also coincided with a reawakening of interest in black and white photography. Few fortunes are made in this rather specialised market, though it can be satisfying to know that your pictures are being bought on aesthetic qualities alone. (Photograph: Colin Leftley)

You will never be able to work on more than one or two projects at any one time, but a notebook full of ideas can act as a prompt at times when energy and motivation are in short supply. Times when it's not possible to be producing pictures can be put to research. Local papers and periodicals will give advance publicity to forthcoming events; anything that looks interesting should be entered in a diary. Tourist offices are excellent sources of useful information;

they will have brochures on public events, beauty spots and places of interest, historic buildings, stately homes, etc.

Public events — such as traction-engine rallies, custom-car meetings, air displays and outings of old steam trains — may produce saleable pictures. The trouble is that the world and his wife are toting cameras on these occasions, and it may be virtually impossible to take any shots that don't include other photographers. It may be better to chat with people and take a few names and addresses.

A vintage car is impossible to photograph properly when it's lined up with hundreds of others in a field, but the owner may be sufficiently flattered by your interest to let you photograph it on another occasion in more sympathetic surroundings. Don't always take the easy option; hold out for pictures that are worthwhile, imaginative and — ultimately — saleable.

The Written Word

It's an oft-quoted cliché that a picture is worth a thousand words. And you could make a convincing argument that a good picture can stand on its own without being buttressed by text or captions. Yet, outside a gallery context, pictures and words go naturally together to present the reader with a complete package of information.

Any photographer who can string words together convincingly will immediately find more opportunities open to him than the photographer who supplies pictures alone. Magazine editors, for example, are always interested in illustrated articles and features. And all photographers will need to write quite lengthy picture captions from time to time. Even the letters accompanying photographic submissions should be clear and literate. It's expensive for magazines to dispatch both a writer *and* a photographer to cover a feature or story, so someone who can adequately combine the two roles will always be in demand.

The most common advice in these circumstances is that you should write as you speak. Knowing the way that most of us speak, this seems poor advice indeed. And photographers, when they put their minds to it, are capable of producing gobbledegook that even a civil servant might envy. You only have to look at photographers' statements in exhibition catalogues to find that they happily reproduce the worst literary excesses of the fine-art world. It doesn't matter whether we are writing about pictures or plumbing, pretentious waffle should have no place.

Some photographers take a perverse delight in being illiterate, as though an inability to use words might somehow increase their kudos as makers and takers of images. But for most editorial uses pictures have to be combined with text and, at least, they have to be furnished with captions that are appropriate to the market.

The photographer who specialises in social and public relations

Every picture may tell a story but, as likely as not, it won't be the *whole* story. Most pictures require some sort of written caption, though the exact form that caption should take depends on the market or publication being supplied. A sporting magazine will want a number of details to back up a picture such as this one: the teams taking part, the name of the competition, venue, final score, etc. There may be a more personal, human-interest story about one of the players which might appeal to a local paper. Such a picture might be used in a national paper, to head a general article on competitive sports. Since it sums up the essence of Rugby football, it might make a saleable stock picture, in which case the caption might be a model of brevity.

One thing is for certain: the time to note down captions is at the time a picture is taken. A busy photographer will find it hard, after a few weeks have gone by, to remember exactly when and where a picture was shot. It can be made less of a chore by carrying a note pad and pen — or even a micro-tape recorder — in the gadget bag. (Photograph: Malc Birkitt)

work, for example, will take pains to identify every person in every picture and give a brief outline of the event concerned. The sports photographer will do likewise; a stunning picture of a motor-bike race meeting will be of no interest to the bike magazines without the names of the competitors, and where they finished in the race. While this information will not be of overriding importance to the

187

editor of a photographic magazine, he *will* want technical details that are pertinent to his readers.

Landscape photographs need precise details of locations. Don't wait until the box of slides lands on the doormat; carry a notebook or micro-tape recorder and record all relevant details at the time you shoot your pictures. This will save headaches and mistakes later on, since our memories are seldom as good as we think they are.

There are other considerations to keep in mind when writing picture captions. It's surprisingly easy to give offence to the people in your pictures by providing misleading captions. If you really put your foot in it you may even attract a libel suit. It is generally accepted that photographers have the legal right to photograph freely in public places. But photographers must shoulder a number of responsibilities when these pictures are eventually published. You may, for example, have taken an unobjectionable photograph of people drinking in a pub, but problems can arise when that picture is used with an article about, say, alcohol abuse. Your picture suddenly takes on a different aspect if the caption intimates that it portrays heavy drinkers who are putting their health at risk. If one of the subjects in your photograph is known to be a teetotaller, and what appears to be gin in his glass is actually only mineral water, then he will claim, rightly, that his character has been defamed.

It is up to the photographer to ensure that his pictures and captions do not present a misleading impression. It's easy to become complacent about the way your pictures are used, since in ninety-nine cases out of a hundred no offence is caused. Be constantly vigilant that captions give an honest reading of what was happening in the pictures.

Model releases

Whenever possible, get the subjects in your pictures to sign a model release: a standard form which helps to clarify the working relationship between the photographer and his models. On the form can be entered any fee that the photographer has paid, and the presence of the model's signature will preclude claims to any further payment. If there are any stipulations on the use of the photographs (eg, not for advertising), then this too can be itemised on the model release form. The form thus acts as a legally binding contract and safeguard for both parties.

It is not a very big step from writing captions to writing short features which will amplify a single photograph or picture story.

Young journalists have long been drilled to ask five relevant questions when interviewing or researching a story: who? what? where? when? why? This can take a form as brief as a single-sentence caption, or be expanded into a full-blown article.

For speculative submissions to magazines the combination of pictures *and* text gives an editor material which he can use immediately, once a sub-editor has licked the words into shape. You have to appreciate that deadlines are always pressing; there just may be no time for the editor to get someone to write suitable text to accompany your pictures. Even a phone call to the photographer with a request for back-up text will create a further delay. However good your pictures may be, they may be rejected simply because it would take too long to assemble a suitable feature.

You have, for example, a selection of photographs which illustrate the way that special-effects filters can be used. The editor of a photographic magazine may find them intriguing enough to

As a postscript to a book about making money from photography, here is the author signing off with an almost unsaleable picture, taken with the aid of a sparkler left over from bonfire night, a tripod-mounted camera, flashgun, long exposure, a few friends and the kind of instant inspiration that comes naturally once the pubs have shut. It's good to remember that photography is about enjoyment as well as putting cheques in the bank. So have fun . . .

hang onto, hoping to slot some of them into his magazine when the topic of filters next crops up on the editorial agenda. But if you'd described exactly how you used filters to get your shots, the editor might have been able to run your pictures right away.

Don't worry that your text isn't quite up to Booker-prize standards; just present the facts of your story as clearly as possible. Any shortcomings of style or presentation will be tidied up by one of the magazine's staff.

Useful Addresses

Space precludes a long listing of useful addresses for the freelance photographer, but most can be found in *The Writers' and Artists' Yearbook*.

The Bureau of Freelance Photographers, Focus House, 497 Green Lanes, London N13 4BP. Members receive regular market newsletters and surveys. Also produces the BFP Course in Freelance Photography and Photo-journalism.

Steepleprint Ltd, 5 Mallard Close, Earls Barton, Northampton NN6 0LS. Printers of 'Able-Labels', printed self-adhesive stickers useful for identifying prints, slides, etc.

Walkerprint, 46 Newman Street, London W1P 3PA. Printers of photographers' index cards; distribution to agencies if required.

Further Reading

The Writers' and Artists' Yearbook. £5.50, published by A. & C. Black (Publishers) Ltd, 35 Bedford Row, London WC1R 4JH. An indispensable annual handbook, which contains much useful information for photographers: listings of magazines (both UK and major overseas markets), publishers, markets for photographers, picture libraries and agencies, photographic societies, etc.

The Directory of Exhibition Spaces, edited by Neil Hanson and Susan Jones. £5.95, published by Arctic Producers Publishing Company Ltd, PO Box 23, Old Simpson Street School, Simpson Street, Sunderland SR4 6DG. A useful directory for artists and photographers, with a comprehensive listing of places to exhibit work.

The Freelance Photographer's Market Handbook, edited by John Tracy and Stewart Gibson. £6.95, published by BFP Books, Focus House, 497 Green Lanes, London N13 4BP. An annual handbook, currently listing over 700 different markets for photographers, including magazines, cards, calendars and picture libraries, plus addresses of photographic services and suppliers.

Pictures That Sell, by Ray Daffurn and Roger Hicks. £12.95, published by Collins, 8 Grafton Street, London W1X 3LA. An excellent guide to the shooting and selling of stock photography through picture libraries.

The Perfect Portfolio, by Henrietta Brackman. £15.95, published by Columbus Books, Devonshire House, 29 Elmfield Road, Bromley, Kent, BR1 1LT.

Index